THE STEMPUNK PROJECT

TRENT FOWLER

Acknowledgements

I designed the STEMpunk Project almost entirely on my own, so I don't have one of those lengthy multi-page acknowledgement sections you find at the beginning of serious scholarly works. Like everyone else my willingness to tackle such an undertaking and the eventual manner in which I did so owes much to conversations I've had over the years. They say you're the average of the five people you spend the most time with; I think that's an enormous oversimplification, but there is the ring of truth about it. Because I have always tried hard to surround myself with people who share my sense of life, my enthusiasm for self-improvement, and my thirst for knowledge I had no trouble getting guidance when I needed it.

But I would be remiss if I didn't single out 6.5 people for special thanks[1]. First, Jeffrey Biles, who is one of my oldest and longest-standing friends. There are no two ways about: Jeffrey was absolutely vital to the success of the STEMpunk Project. He was the first person I talked to about it, back when it had an entirely different name, and he was an inexhaustible source of advice, inspiration, and support. Second, Brian Ziman. Brian knows as much about STEM subjects as any three people I've met, and never shied away from tutoring me in computer design, Arduino programming, artificial intelligence, and a million other subjects. Third, Erik Istre. The stress of finishing a PhD project and moving back to North America meant that Erik didn't have much time to spend consulting for the STEMpunk Project. But he did provide thoughtful commentary on

---

[1] In addition to those mentioned, the cover was designed by the excellent art deco artist Rodolfo Reyes, and the sigils at the beginning of each section are the work of SigilDaily.com

the manuscript, and I would estimate that 98% of everything I know about mathematics comes from the fact that he was good natured enough to try and teach logic and set theory to a chimpanzee like myself. Fourth, my college buddy Richard Pears took a break from his duties as an elected official in Britain to read my humble treatise and offer suggestions. Fifth, Wayne Radinsky of the Boulder Future Salon not only pointed out errors in an early draft of this book, but has also been encouraging me since all those years ago when I first offered to speak on artificial intelligence in Boulder, Colorado.

In a completely different way I owe a debt of gratitude to my fiancé Brenda Chacon, who was my support team and cheerleader along the way. She alone was there to make me coffee at 4:30 in the morning and to tell me she believed in me when I grew frustrated at repeated setbacks. This would've been a much lonelier road without her.

Finally, I should acknowledge the newest addition to my life, my daughter Genevieve. I would never have guessed that I could learn so much from a tiny little micro-human who is barely a month old. But I have. I hope someday she reads this book, and feels the same desire to rise as her father does.

Trent Fowler

July 14, 2017

Introduction

As I sit writing this exactly a year has passed since I began a project to teach myself as much about computer science, electronics, mechanics, and artificial intelligence as possible. In the service of this quest I have torn apart broken fans and pumps to inspect their internal components, read circuit diagrams, watched videos on induction motors, subpanels, transmissions, and batteries, worked with SparkFun electronics kits to make LED bulbs flash when buttons are pushed, devoured textbooks on AI, computer science fundamentals, and mechanical engineering, picked up a soldering iron, and written code. My facility with the relevant concepts and techniques has improved dramatically as a result.

Throughout the project I have described my efforts as an attempt to reduce the number of 'black boxes' in my life. But I am not one of those people whose fascination wanes as uncertainties sublimate into understanding. The majesty of stars is not lessened by the knowledge that they are plasma titans hurling thermonuclear fury into the vast reaches of interstellar space. And this is doubly true for man-made artifacts such as engines.

Like everyone else I get so caught up in the vicissitudes of life that I fail to notice the quotidian machinery which makes it possible. But thanks to the STEMpunk project I also have lucid moments when I am awestruck at the intricacy and power of that machinery. Sometimes I pop the hood of my car to search for the source of a new and unwelcome noise; sometimes I pop the hood of my car to admire the frozen crystal of deliberate thought which lies beneath.

Though this project has decreased the amount of *mystery* in the world, it has not decreased the amount of *magic*.

And for that reason, the struggle has been worth it.

Inevitably in a project of this scale one learns as much about the learning process as about the subject matter, especially when it is self-structured and self-motivated. And in fact a sizeable fraction of the blogging I've done throughout has been devoted to issues like staying focused and bouncing back from failure.

So this book has been divided into two sections. The 'Metacraft' section goes into detail on the difficult task of learning a lot in a very short time. In chapter 1 I discuss strategies for approaching tacit knowledge, which consists of hands-on acumen that isn't usually written down anywhere. Chapter 2 is devoted to mantra stacks and visualizations, which I found useful in staying motivated through-out. Chapter 3 is about focused, deep work. Chapter 4 debuts the term 'ultrapraxist', which I coined for scholars like Cal Newport who are exceptional because they are really, really good at working effectively. I did something similar in chapter 5, which discusses the cognitive state I call 'semignosis'. Chapter 6 is my obligatory treatment of entity theory and incremental theory and the profound ramifications they have for how individuals process success and failure.

The STEMpunk section discusses the project itself, including such topics as how I chose to structure my studies, what sorts of problems I encountered, and what I learned about the subject matter along the way. Chapters 7 and 8 of this section are essential reading for anyone interested in designing a large-scale learning project of their own; chapters 9, 10, and 11 contain detailed accounts of what I learned about computing, electronics, and mechanics (respectively) as well as essays on random topics within those disciplines in the style of Isaac Asimov's old popular science books. The final chapter is a philosophical look at the ways in which this project has enriched my view of the world.

While my generous friends helped enormously to improve this book, I did not have access to a professional technical editor. Moreover,

I'm not an expert in these subjects, just an amateur trying to better understand the world. As such I'm sure there are probably numerous errors remaining in the text. Please feel free to reach out to me with any corrections through my personal blog: https://rulersto-thesky.com/about/

—

Alas, the map is not the territory and words can never fully capture experiences. But I do hope you are inspired to tackle your own learning projects. While I've always believed that a life spent learning is a life well-lived, this is the first time I've ever taken on such an ambitious challenge.

May it not be the last.

Metacraft

Chapter 1
Approaching Tacit Knowledge

For any new skill, whether it be carpentry or musical composition, there is always a gap between what an expert is able to explain and what they are able to do. This gap has many names, but one of the most common is 'tacit knowledge', defined as that subset of knowledge gained through many years interacting with a set of problems and the various approaches for solving them.

Tacit knowledge is the reason that apprenticeship must accompany study: there is much which even a master has difficulty writing down or communicating at all.

For any given domain it is often the case that symptoms underdetermine their causes. There are lots of reasons why an engine might start making an unusual noise, and the reason might be impossible to pin down without quite a bit of forensic work. An expert is able to deal with this indeterminacy in two ways: first, there are often patterns in the data which aren't detectable by the novice. Engine 'noise' might be subtly different for timing belt issues and busted seals, for example. Second, experience in a field begins to impart a vague 'sense' for what the most likely causes are for common and uncommon problems. It may be the case that a certain symptom has three possible causes, but one of them is *vastly* more common than the others, so that's where the expert always starts.

Tacit knowledge needn't be confined just to knowledge of a specific set of tasks, but can extend to an entire lore known and shared within a wider community of enthusiasts. In 'The Case for Working With Your Hands', Matthew Crawford provides the example of 'Fred', an extremely experienced motorcycle mechanic who was able to diagnose an engine failure because he knew about the kinds of metals used to manufacture a minor component in Honda motorcycles from the 1970's[2].

I would venture to guess *that* information isn't available anywhere except in the brains of people like Fred. In addition to this kind of arcane minutia, tacit knowledge can also take the form of a 'feel' for problems and their solutions. The chances are good that a skilled programmer is using information available to anyone for free on the internet, but knowing where to find it and when to apply it requires patience and practice.

Fields can be categorized as more 'experiential' or more 'conceptual', with the defining feature being how much of the relevant knowledge can be gained from books versus apprenticeship. Physics is a highly conceptual field insofar as most of it can be learned from a textbook. Plumbing is a highly experiential field insofar as much of the knowledge required to be a good plumber must be learned on the job with your sleeves rolled up.

To be sure this boundary isn't a hard one -- physicists need experience and plumbers need concepts[3]. But if we accept this distinction then we must face experiential and conceptual fields in the manner that their nature demands. We may crack open the books for a conceptual field, but an experiential field requires a different approach.

I've worked with a number of talented craftsmen and they're often not very good at explaining what they're doing and why[4]. I don't

---

[2] P. 108

[3] Electricians, plumbers, and other tradespeople have to have a comprehensive knowledge of building standards, coding requirements, and so forth. Even so, I think my distinction is a useful one.

[4] As a possible alternative solution to this problem one of my beta readers recommended 'Asking The Right Questions' by Browne and Keeley

know the reason for this, but as a result I've attempted to develop ways of more quickly mastering tacit knowledge independently. Two techniques have resulted from these efforts: 'failure autopsies' and 'insight mining'.

A failure autopsy is a detailed analysis of an error cascade not unlike the tapes made by professional athletes which are used to reflect upon and improve game-time performance. This analogy fails in a few interesting ways because the mind is harder to observe and direct than the body, but it's the same idea. Here's how it works:

1) List out the bare steps of whatever it was you were doing, mistakes and successes alike.

2) Identify the points at which mistakes were made.

3) Categorize the nature of those mistakes.

4) Repeatedly visualize yourself making the correct judgment, at the actual location, if possible.

5) (Optional) explicitly try to either analogize this context to others where the same mistake may occur, or develop toy models of the error cascade which you can use to template onto possible future contexts.

No doubt an example or two will make this clearer. In 2016 I spent an afternoon working with an employee to troubleshoot the air conditioners for a large shop building. There were two five-ton AC units outside, each of which was connected to a wall-mounted thermostat inside the room. Neither of us were HVAC technicians[5] and neither of us had much of any idea what the problem was. Here is a short version of what we did to try and resolve the issue:

1) Notice that the right thermostat is malfunctioning.

---

[5] Someone else was in the process of contacting an actual technician, and we were doing what we could until one was available

2) Decide to turn both AC units off[6] at the breaker[7] instead of at the thermostat.

3) Decide to change the batteries in both thermostats.

4) Take both thermostats off the wall at the same time, in order to change their batteries.

5) Instruct employee to carry both thermostats to the house where the batteries are stored. This involves going outside into the cold.

The only non-mistakes were steps 1) and 3), with every other step involving an error of some sort. Here is my analysis:

*2a) We didn't first check to see if the actual unit was working; we just noticed the thermostat was malfunctioning and skipped straight to taking action. I call this a *Grounding Failure* because we failed to establish any kind of a baseline by taking a step back and looking at the problem as a whole.

*2b) We decided to turn both units off at the breaker, but it never occurred to us that abruptly cutting off power might stress some of the internal components of the air conditioner. I call this *implication blindness* or *implicasia*. The term 'implicasia' is a deliberate reference to the medical term 'aphasia' which denotes an inability to understand or formulate speech as a result of brain damage.

---

[6] Why even consider turning off a functioning AC? The interior of the garage has a lot of heavy machinery in it and thus gets pretty warm, especially on hot days, and if the ACs run continuously eventually the freon circulating lines will frost over and the unit will shut down. So, if you know the units have been working hard all day it's often wise to manually shut one or both units down for ten minutes to make sure the lines have a chance to defrost and then manually turn them back on.

[7] Why even consider shutting off an AC at the breaker instead of the thermostat? The same reason that you sometimes have to shut an entire computer down and turning it back on when troubleshooting. Sometimes you have no idea what's wrong, so a restart is the only reasonable next step.

*2c) Turning both units off at the same time, instead of doing one and then the other, introduced extra variables that made downstream diagnostic efforts muddier and harder to perform. I call this *increasing causal opacity (ICO)*.

*4) We took both thermostats off the wall at the same time. It never occurred to us that thermostat position might matter, i.e. that putting the right thermostat in the slot where the left used to go or vice versa might be problematic, so this is *implicasia*. Further, taking both down at the same time is *ICO*.

*5) Taking warm thermostats outside on a frigid night might cause water to condense on the inside, damaging the electrical components. This possibility didn't occur to me (*implicasia*).

Interventions

So far all this amounts to is a tedious analysis of an unfolding disaster. What I did after I got this down on paper was try and relive each step, visualizing myself performing the correct mental action.

This begins with noticing that the thermostat is malfunctioning. In my simulation I'm looking at the thermostat with my employee, we see the failure, and the first thought that pops into my simulated head is to have him go outside and determine whether or not the AC unit is working.

I repeat this step a few times, performing repetitions the same way I might do in the gym.

Next, in my simulation I assume that the unit was not working (remember that in real life we never checked and don't know), and so I simulate having two consecutive thoughts: 'let's shut down just the one unit, so as not to increase causal opacity' and 'but we'll start at the thermostat instead of at the breaker, so that the unit shuts down slowly before we cut power altogether. I don't want to fall victim to implicasia and assume an abrupt shut-down won't mess something up'.

The second part of the second thought is important. I don't know that turning an AC off at the breaker will hurt anything, but the point is that I don't know that it won't, which means I should proceed with caution.

As with before I repeat this visualization five times or so.

Finally, I perform this operation with both *d) and *e), in each case imagining myself having the kinds of thoughts that would have resulted in success rather than failure.

A while later I did the same analysis with a different failure, but that time I made a handy flow chart:

(Refer back to this as you read the text below)

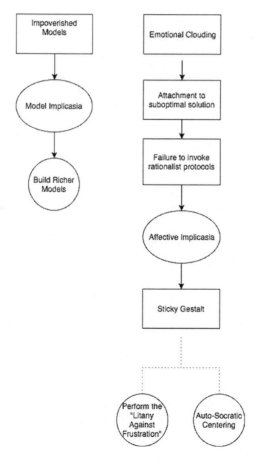

A friend of mine and I had diagnosed a problem with a door knob in the basement of my house. We had taken part of the doorknob out of the door and realized that one of the internal components was stripped. Alas, we were unable to get the knob's tongue to retract, which prevented us from opening the door enough to put in a re-placement knob.

We reasoned that there must be a latch holding the tongue in place. But because we weren't sure we didn't know if we could pry the tongue back without damaging it, if there might be a special release pin only accessible from one side, etc. In other words, we didn't know much about how doorknobs are repaired, which is why *impoverished models* is at the top of one branch of the flow chart.

I call implication blindness arising from impoverished models *model implicasia*, and the solution is to build a better understanding of how a system works. In the case of the doorknob this would probably involve Googling and watching some Youtube videos.

(Protip: that's the solution to *most* problems.)

As this deceptively simple project became more and more difficult I began to grow frustrated. I'm no great handyman but I can solve most common household problems, so when one comes along that's too difficult it's hard not to feel like a helpless, incompetent fool. This lead to *emotional clouding* -- the top of the second branch of the flowchart.

When I become frustrated to this degree I often choose one of the first solutions to come to mind and attach myself to it. I don't recall exactly what bright idea we had come up with, but I believe we were contemplating taking the door off its hinges. Even among subop-timal solutions that's an absolutely terrible notion. But the bigger problem was that emotional clouding meant that I was no longer even *trying* to think like a problem-solving rationalist. Instead my fury was growing blacker with each passing second, bringing me no closer to a workaround.

Implicasia arising from poisonous emotional states is *affective implicasia* and can give rise to a *sticky gestalt*. 'Gestalt' is a word which roughly means 'whole' or 'entirety'. When you look at a friend's face you don't see a mouth, eyes, ears, and a nose, you see a *face* -- the whole thing, as a single gestalt, which you can break down into components if you so choose.

When you've reached a point where your emotions have caused a problem to fuse into a nasty, unworkable mass then you're facing a sticky gestalt. I struggle quite a lot with this, but I have developed some techniques to mitigate it. The first is what I call the 'Litany Against Frustration'. If you've ever read Frank Herbert's towering classic *Dune* then you probably recall the 'Litany Against Fear':

'I must not fear.
Fear is the mind-killer.
Fear is the little-death that brings total obliteration.
I will face my fear.
I will permit it to pass over me and through me.
And when it has gone past I will turn the inner eye to see its path.
Where the fear has gone there will be nothing. Only I will remain.'

My Litany Against Frustration goes like this:

'I notice that I am frustrated.
Frustration is not at all times wrong but in this moment it hinders.
As the fog clears and lays bare the world so too does my frustration dissipate,
leaving me to think and to act.'

With some practice I was able to make this a probable standard response to mounting frustration. Once I've said this a few times it's much easier to step back and view the problem with fresher eyes. (I will have more to say about this and similar techniques in a later chapter.)

Another technique which works in a similar way to clear my head is to engage in *auto-socratic centering*. The ancient Greek philosopher Socrates is famous for his question-based method of teaching. Instead of lecturing on a philosophical topic he would ask his students a long series of questions, during which gaps in their understanding could be revealed, explored, and corrected. Modern philosophy teachers sometimes use this *Socratic method* to guide students toward building their own answers to questions as opposed to simply telling them what they should believe.

Auto-Socratic centering is a bit more restricted. When I've fallen to affective implicasia sometimes it helps to pause for a moment and ask myself questions like:

'what am I doing?',
'what problem am I trying to fix?',
'what issues have I identified?',
'what solutions have I tried and why didn't they work?'

This practice simultaneously lets me calm myself by taking a detached, dispassionate stance toward the problem while also letting me turn things over in my head. Often times something important was overlooked in the angry rush to find a solution.

Once this has been accomplished I try to *reason from local first principles*. This just means I try to break up the sticky gestalt; instead of seeing 'a broken doorknob' I try to see 'a handle, a tongue, at least one latch, a slot for the tongue which keeps the door from opening...' and so on. Even if this doesn't lead to a solution it makes the process much less frustrating and makes it easier to communicate clearly with someone who might be able to help.

If a failure autopsy is a way of maximizing learning from inevitable failures, *insight mining* is a variation meant to maximize learning from successful projects led by people more experienced than yourself.

This past summer I was helping to refurbish an attic and about twice an hour the carpenter with whom I was working deployed some ingenious trick which I know I would never have thought of on my own. At one point we were installing an intake fan to move cool, dry air from outside into the attic, which was too hot and humid to work in ninety-nine percent of the time. Doing this requires cutting two identical holes in a wall -- one on the inside and one on the outside.

How would *you* have done this?

One obvious solution is to take careful measurements of how far off the ground the center of one circle is, and then to measure the same distance on the other side of the wall before making the cut. But if you're working in an attic that means there's at least one floor beneath you, and probably some furniture and other obstacles beneath that. Instead, the head carpenter made a circle on one side of the wall, then took an extra-long drill bit and drilled into the center of the circle and through the wall to the other side. Then, someone standing outside just drew a circle of the same radius with the drill bit at the center.

That's pretty clever. After the project was done I took a list of these little insights and mulled them over, imagining myself using similar hacks in future projects. This is how I get as much as possible from working with superior craftsmen.

As far as I know both failure autopsies and insight mining are unique to me. I have spent some time talking to the kinds of researchers who might know of similar techniques and have found no leads. If anyone reading this has pursued similar lines of thinking I would be glad to know about it.

When virtual reality becomes sophisticated and cheap enough it's likely that novices will be trained on simulations of actual tasks within their respective fields. Until then, these are the quickest ways I know to acquire tacit knowledge.

Chapter 2

Mantra Stacks

Throughout the STEMpunk Project I experimented with different protocols for designing mantras and visualization exercises, combining them into 'stacks' like one might do with nootropics, and nestling them into ritual structures which make them more likely to become habits. As a result I was afforded the opportunity to explore this territory under a variety of conditions, both favorable and unfavorable, and I feel prepared to discuss my findings.

My hypothesis is that these techniques work because they create mental 'grooves' towards which attention, energy, and motivation flow. It's one thing to say you want to start waking up earlier, and quite another to develop a mantra around rising at dawn and spending ten minutes each day visualizing yourself doing so. This invests the goal of becoming a morning person with a psychological gravity that a simple affirmation doesn't, making it more likely that you'll be able to follow through[8].

Traditionally these techniques would have been deployed in a religious, not secular, context. Some cognitive operations are best performed via what I call the *mythopoetic command line interface* -- which works like an actual command line interface but in the language of dreams, symbols, art, and metaphor -- and religions have

---

[8] This probably isn't even close to the full story, but it seems a useful enough metaphor for present purposes and not obviously wrong in any way, so it will be my point of departure.

always had a monopoly on this[9]. The ritual apparatus and introspective scaffolding religions provide are important in the difficult task of shaping a human being.

That having been said there is no dogma or metaphysical commitment associated with the exercises I describe below. To the best of my knowledge they are compatible with existing religious beliefs and with an absence of such belief.

The First Steps

When I began I did two mantra sessions daily: one in the morning and one at night. They were structured as follows:

Morning:

Lit a candle, took a few deep breaths.

[Spoken aloud]:

'Initiate Titan Bootstrap Sequence'

[Spoken aloud]:

'I will be like water in my process,
earth in my resolve,
fire in my intensity,
and air in my presence'.
(This mantra is henceforth 'The element meditation'.)

---

[9] It has been pointed out to me that this analogy could be taken further by analogizing religions as apps, which are sleek and prefabricated but also try you in the confines of their designer's intentions. The mythopoetic CLI would take more time to learn but reward the effort many times over in flexibility and power.

[Spoken aloud]:

'I notice that I am distracted.
A mind that wanders is not at all times wrong,
but in this moment, it hinders.
As the colors of a prism become like a knife when focused,
so too does the light of my mind converge upon the task at hand.'
(This mantra is henceforth 'The Litany Against Distraction'.)

[Written]:

Some habit mantra. Generally these consisted of a short phrase that I would write longhand between 15-25 times. An example: 'I will spend my last hour reading by candlelight'.

[Visualized]:

The best version of the coming day that I could imagine, with a special emphasis on moving quickly and efficiently from task to task.

Night:

Lit a candle and took a few deep breaths.

[Spoken aloud]:

'Initiate Titan shutdown sequence'.
The element meditation, same as before.

[Spoken aloud]:

'I notice that I am frustrated.
Frustration is not at all times wrong,
but in this moment, it hinders.
As the fog clears and lays bare the world so too does my frustration dissipate,
leaving me to think and to act.'
(This mantra is henceforth 'The Litany Against Frustration'. You may remember it from chapter 6.)

[Written]:

Some habit mantra, usually about getting up early the next day.

[Spoken aloud]:

'if/then's, i.e. 'if I wake up tired, then I will still get up'.

Some of this may seem grandiose and overblown. Is it really necessary to begin with a phrase like 'Initiate Titan Bootstrap Sequence'? Surely I don't consider myself a Titan, after all, and what purpose is served by styling myself after the four classical elements?

Perhaps the more interesting part of the answer to that question is that many aspects of the mantra stack just occurred to me. Once I began tinkering with my practice phrases began suggesting themselves as natural extensions of what I was already doing. I still remember how the element meditation kept coming to mind, almost fully formed, until I finally decided to incorporate it into the stack.

The same is true of the opening phrase, 'Initiate Titan Bootstrap Sequence'. After a few days it just felt like I needed a dedicated signal to myself that the mantra stack was beginning, and as soon as I noticed this feeling the sentence presented itself to me.

Furthermore, as time went on some of the mantras became accompanied by stylized hieroglyphic images. These days when I say the Litany Against Distraction I picture a man standing with a rainbow beginning about a foot behind him at eye level, the colors converging as they pass through his head to become a focused point of searing light about a foot in front of him. This too was something that occurred naturally and with little overt effort.

The rest of the answer is that I believe the best mantras have a solemn, lyrical quality that echoes other elements of the religious memeplex. Commandments, poetry, songs, and stories from religious traditions often feel like a cross between a haiku and an aphorism. They are weighty, but short and easy to memorize.

They're true, but general enough to be applicable across vast swaths of a person's life.

They are at once the bow and the arrow; a vast weight with a lever to move it; a linguistic seed that contains an enormous folded structure than opens when fed on sun and rain.

In other words, my mantras sound portentous because that's how mantras are supposed to sound.

Evolution

As the months passed this stack received all number of stress fractures and consequently underwent many changes. For a little while I tried adding a third mantra session around noon, and even gave thought to mimicking the Islamic Salah by doing five sessions a day. At various times I experimented with including failure autopsies in the stack, and was happy with the results.

There's an interesting idea lurking here: I would've loved to have had a program into which I could enter various parameters and time constraints for a given day and received back a customized mantra stack. Even better would be if the program could use data from Thync[10] or something similar to automatically adjust my stack when I'm feeling more frustrated or stressed.

Alas, with an increasingly busy schedule my practice gradually eroded until, these days, I usually just do the initiation sequence and the element meditation each morning. And I'll be honest, I've begun to feel less focused, less centered, and a lot more irritable. Multiple daily sessions would likely be more sustainable if each session is very short, on the order of 90 seconds. That's not enough time to write anything but it is enough to light a candle, do a little chanting, and hopefully get most of the benefit out of the exercise. One or two sessions a day could be longer, and it is during these times that one should do the writing and habit work.

---

[10]   http://www.thync.com/

What Have I Learned?

There are a two important takeaways here. The first is that mantras are definitely effective. More than once I have found myself on the verge of losing my temper only to have the Litany Against Frustration play itself in my head, and the less I've worked through the stack the more often frustration has gotten the better of me.

The second is that my stack naturally bifurcated into theoretical and applied segments. The theoretical side consists of the bootstrap sequence, the two litanies, and the element meditation. These are very abstract, not even remotely specific, and are more about reaffirming a worldview. Thus they are spoken while staring into candlelight and visualizing an associated hieroglyphic instead of being written down, which would take too long. The practical side consists of habits I'm trying to instill, and they are usually written long-hand in front of a candle while I visualize myself performing the action.

The above classification scheme can be usefully extended. The theoretical elements in the mantra stack are like 'rudders' you can attach to an iceberg to do something vaguely like steering. The practical elements can be further categorized as 'vice wedges' or 'skyhooks' in that they distance you from a bad habit or let you reach toward a good one, respectively.

Let me explain that last sentence: in 'Deep Work' Cal Newport recommends waiting five minutes to get online when you really need a piece of information. This small temporal distance diminishes the reward signal you get from distraction, making it less tempting in the future. It drives a wedge between you and your vices. Skyhooks on the other hand are built for ascendancy, and can include any positive behavior you are trying to make into a habit.

Vectors, surfaces, features

Now that we've discussed mantra stacks as a promising way of instilling habits let us turn to a higher-level discussion of purposive action in general.

Physicists are notorious for their impatience with outsiders who misuse concepts from their discipline, so I hope any physicists reading this will forgive me for what I'm about to say. In physics a distinction is made between 'scalar' and 'vector' quantities[11]. A scalar quantity does not have a directional component, and includes measurements such as length, pressure, volume, area, and temperature. A vector quantity necessarily includes a direction, and includes measurements such as velocity, lift, momentum, and acceleration.

I would argue that purposive action begins with *goal vectors* which necessarily contain a directional component -- something towards which the agent is moving. Goals often begin as vague images of some desirable future state, such as having lost fifty pounds or started a business. To be useful they must be decomposed into an *action thread*, a sequence of steps that moves the agent along the vector implied by the goal.

Of course an action thread is made up of discrete behaviors like 'have eggs for breakfast instead of a bagel and cream cheese'. I suspect that a sizeable fraction of failed attempts to achieve a goal occur because people never take the step of decomposing a goal vector into an action thread. But without an understanding of a goal's direction and action thread the desirable future state remains shimmering in the distance, as unreal and unreachable as a mirage.

In a number of places throughout my writings on the STEMpunk Project I have discussed desirable future states I had wanted to attain, like 'reducing the number of black boxes in my life' or 'understanding basic electronics'. The only reason I was successful was because I spent quite a lot of time thinking about which action thread would allow me to accomplish these goals. I can't stress enough how important it is to concretize the steps implied by a goal vector.

Goals are very rarely held in isolation; any given person usually has several things they're going after. When viewed in their entirety a set of goals elucidates the contours of a *motivation surface* -- a broad orientation implied by an agent's behavior.

---

[11]   https://www.grc.nasa.gov/www/k-12/airplane/vectors.html

Arguably the most basic motivation surface would be 'survival', which is common to every form of life. In my framework this is too broad to be a standalone goal[12], even when concretized, and instead functions more like a supergoal driving the formation and pursuit of innumerable subgoals and their respective action threads.

The foregoing may seem to imply that I think human minds are neater than they actually are, but this isn't the case. I know full well that people often pursue goals they don't even realize they have (and may fail to achieve them for reasons they never understand), that people often profess to have goals which they don't even pretend to try to accomplish, that people may have a number of mutually exclusive goals (like 'be in shape' and 'have an active social life which involves frequent consumption of sugary alcoholic beverages'), that people often engage in behaviors which they know to be destructive, and so on.

With this in mind I want to introduce the notion of *consonant* and *dissonant* motivation surfaces. A consonant motivation surface is one whose goal vectors are either pointed in the same direction or, at a minimum, not actively interfering with each other. A dissonant motivation structure, on the other hand, comprises goals which cannot be achieved at the same time. Some people can drink heavily and often without gaining weight, but I am not one of them. So if my social life involves lots of drinking *and* I want to stay in shape then my motivation surface has become dissonant[13].

I see no reason why an agent couldn't act to introduce more consonance into their motivation surfaces, especially once they have concepts like 'action threads' and 'goal vectors'. The best way to achieve this would probably be to approach behavior with more intentionality, more *deliberateness*. Spend some time thinking about *why* you're going (or not going) to the gym, cooking less

---

[12] I think a biologist would disagree, but they use a broader definition of 'goal'.

[13] Instead of saying we have one dissonant motivation surface we could say we have *two* motivation surfaces -- one for health and one for social life -- which have become dissonant with respect to one another. I don't think this alternative formulation changes the analysis much.

and eating out more often, spending money when you should be saving it, etc. Maybe you need to concretize your goals as action threads to stay on track more consistently. Or you may have a hidden goal which you're acting to maximize without consciously realizing it. You may crave social approval more than you are willing to admit, which means you're going out more often, drinking more often, spending more money than you want to, and sabotaging your workouts. Knowing is half the battle, as they say, and once you've had this insight you can devise corrective measures.

It's possible to engineer motivation surfaces by continuously pursuing relevant goals. In high school my brother was an overweight gamer who couldn't have been forced to the gym at gunpoint. But over time he came to be fascinated with the world of competitive bodybuilding and has since appeared in several state-level competitions. Ten years ago it would've been inconceivable to me that he would some day be in far better shape than I am, but that's the reality, and I couldn't be prouder of him.

As a matter of fact some of this analysis was inspired by conversations he and I have had. He told me once that he enjoys listening to motivational bodybuilding videos[14] while exercising, not because they impart any new information, but because they keep him motivated and focused. It was around that time that I first began to think about techniques for engineering mental grooves to change default behaviors, and the rest eventually followed.

---

[14] For example: https://www.youtube.com/watch?v=wVW88PQGVBQ

Chapter 3
Focus and Depth

'...[T]he skillfull management of attention is the first step toward any behavioral change and covers most self-improvement approaches like a vast umbrella.'

Winifred Gallagher's 'Rapt' -- the book in which the above quote can be found, on page 10 -- is a breezy, uplifting treatise on attention, that prism through which the light of experience is filtered, refracted, and bent. We live with greater demands on our time and attention than at any previous point in history, and knowing how attention works is paramount for anyone seeking to live the good life. The science in Gallagher's slim NYT-bestseller is elucidated with patient visual metaphors and the prose is sprinkled with ample references from literature, history, and philosophy.

For years I have believed that attention is a poorly understood and deeply important aspect of human cognition. I suspect that it underlies Sapir-Whorf effects[15] and various other cross-cultural psychological differences, and I have noticed that many spectacularly successful people are most strikingly different from the rest of us in that they can enter long periods of deep, sustained focus.

---

[15] Russian speakers are allegedly able to differentiate shades of blue that speakers of other languages can't. It's thought this is because their language differentiates between shades of blue that other languages don't. My view is that a language's communicative apparatus repeatedly draw a speaker's attention to different aspects of reality, perhaps even causing them to perceive things others miss. Anyone could learn to see the different shades, they just haven't yet because their language hasn't forced them to notice.

Gallagher cites Tiger Woods, Admiral Horatio Nelson, and mathematical super-genius Srinivasa Ramanujan as examples of what unwavering attention can achieve.

She also discusses a number of useful conceptual distinctions, one of which is between 'experiential' and 'pragmatic' styles of attention[16]. A person prone to experiential absorption might spontaneously weep at a sunrise because they find it very natural to settle into an expansive state of relaxed concentration. This is very different from a pragmatic style of attention like that used while researching pediatricians or local gyms. Such attention is usually tight, goal-directed, and favored by the sort of executive types who just want to get the job done.

But variations in attention also have profound ramifications for wellbeing. People with a sunny disposition are often simply better at noticing the positive in their life. In a fascinating set of studies professor Richard Wiseman discovered that one of the things distinguishing profoundly lucky people from profoundly unlucky people was that the former tended to see silver linings in otherwise sinister cloud fronts[17]. This is a skill that can be trained; I make it a semi-regular habit to keep a 'gratitude journal', wherein I write about things for which I am thankful.

The operative mechanism here is that at each moment it's impossible to notice more than a tiny fraction of the world's innumerable facets, meaning that we are all engaged in a constant shifting of our attentional priorities. It's as if attention is a flashlight roaming constantly over a landscape, first passing over a bend in a river, then a fallen tree, then birds taking flight, and so on. If your flashlight is more prone to fall on scenes of carnage and despair, you'll wind up morose. If all you ever see are daisies and sunshine, you'll be relatively upbeat.

---

[16] 'Rapt', Winifred Gallagher, p. 58.

[17] There is much more to the story. I highly recommend Wiseman's 'The Luck Factor'.

The good news is that you can change your worldview by changing your view of the world.

Given its role in high achievement and happiness it should be clear that attention is worth understanding and building. At the beginning of May 2016 I devised an experiment to do just that. It began as follows: every day of the week except Sunday was either a 'thick focus day' or a 'thin focus day'. Mondays, Wednesdays, and Fridays were thick focus days and Tuesdays, Thursdays, and Saturdays were thin focus days. Sundays were spent cleaning the house and catching up on chores.

There were several criteria for thick focus days. One, I would meditate during my five-minute Pomodoro breaks. Two, I didn't access the internet until noon[18]. On really busy days I made an exception by having my phone close in case anyone really needed to get in touch with me, but by and large I adhered to this stricture.

Third, I didn't listen to music or podcasts while on short commutes, using the time instead to either reflect on my day or run through mantras. At first I intended to spend all driving time in silence but after a couple of days I eased this rule so that it only applied to trips of less than fifteen minutes. Driving for an entire hour and not listening to an audiobook seemed a little pointless.

I also wanted to exercise without distractions on thick focus days but I workout at a public gym and can't control the radio. Since I have to listen to some music I figured that it may as well be my own.

On thin focus days I would stretch or do calisthenics while taking a break from work. For the most part I used some variant of a quick exercise circuit I've used in the past: fifty jumping jacks, forty situps, thirty pushups, and twenty bodyweight squats. I allowed

---

[18] It's not totally true that I never accessed the internet. I have to have my wifi on to save to Evernote and sync my Anki spaced-repetition software with its internet database. Plus I'd occasionally Google words I didn't know or images to add to flashcards. But I wasn't on social media or checking my email.

myself to listen to music on any commute, but I still didn't access the internet until noon.

This was only supposed to last two weeks but I liked my results and so extended it to fill out the rest of the month. I switched from alternating thick and thin focus days to having thick and thin focus time periods in the same day. Occasionally, when I hadn't gotten enough sleep, meditating during a thick focus day was miserable and I needed to move around a little. Likewise there were times when I was scatter-brained and just wanted to reorient with meditation instead of doing situps.

So I decided to just use my discretion. If I felt tired breaks would be spent getting my blood moving, and if I couldn't focus I'd meditate instead. I still didn't use the internet until late in the morning, and even though I could've listened to anything I wanted to while driving, on most days I chose instead to simply think.

This experiment produced several interesting results. After a few days I felt increasingly reluctant to go back to thin focus days, wanting instead to spend my time working deeply on The STEMpunk Project. While I felt the odd pang of desire to hop on Facebook in the beginning these faded after a day or two, and I eventually started to feel a little disgusted with myself when I gave into this desire, even when it was well into evening.

It consequently became easier to maintain focus while I was washing the dishes or cleaning the bathroom, and I would find myself stopping to meditate for the span of a single breath at random times throughout the day. I smiled more often, was generally less stressed, and was less tempted to drive really fast or listen to really loud music.

Of course stewarding the finite resource of attention doesn't do much good if you're choosing low-value things to focus on. I suppose we could say that *paying* attention (to something or someone) and *spending* attention (to multiple actions along a goal vector over time) are different skills.

Cal Newport's *Deep Work* is an ode to sustained, high-octane focus with unambiguous guidelines for how to spend attention. A brief summary might go like this: 'Some work, like responding to emails and attending meetings is shallow and easily automated. Other work, like proving new results in a field of math, is deep and very difficult to automate. You should do more deep work because it's more valuable.'

Of course this is harder than it sounds. Luckily the second section of Newport's book discusses four overarching rules for working more intentionally in a world that struggles mightily to shatter attention: 'work deeply', 'embrace boredom', 'quit social media', and 'drain the shallows'.

Pursuing depth requires more than a simple resolution to be less distracted. Instead an aspiring deep worker might adopt one of several strategies to get the job done. The computer scientist Donald Knuth, who famously dropped his email address in 1990 to pursue research in cloistered silence, embraces the *monastic strategy*. Most people simply won't have this option because of obligations to earn money, build a career, and provide for a family. But in most cases it will be possible to get periods of deep work by utilizing the *bimodal strategy*. Newport illustrates this approach with Carl Jung, a famous 20th century psychologist who retreated to a stone house in the country to work intensely on new ideas while spending the rest of his time in the hectic rush of professional academia. Bimodal deep workers might have a few weeks or months throughout the year during which they are sealed away from distraction but otherwise attend meeting and answer emails like everyone else.

Even this may not be possible for everyone, in which case a *rhythmic strategy* might be more appropriate. This requires scheduling specific deep-work periods within each day. Because I have extensive professional responsibilities and a daughter on the way this is my preferred method of achieving depth. I like to rise as early as possible, which can vary from 4:30 to 7:30 in the morning, and spend at least an hour working on this book (or some other difficult and high-value task).

The advanced deep worker is free to use the *journalistic strategy* of switching into focus whenever the opportunity arises. Newport discusses famed writer Walter Isaacson's ability to work in stretches of as little as twenty minutes to produce thousand-page biographies while maintaining a thriving career as a writer for *Time* magazine. The journalistic strategy seems to work better for some kinds of deep work than others. I have difficulty believing that anyone could do great mathematics research in twenty minutes; but if the hard thinking is done and all that's left is writing the book, twenty minutes here and there might suffice.

Whether you end up spending months or minutes in undistracted work you'll benefit from greater powers of concentration. This can be trained just like a muscle with techniques like meditation or having 'thick' and 'thin' focus days, but also by simply training yourself to be less addicted to distracting stimuli. Unfortunately most of us have become extremely dependent upon our smartphones to relieve even momentary boredom in our lives. Newport offers a simple corrective: embrace boredom.

Instead of scrolling through your Facebook news feed while in line at the grocery store just stand there and *be bored*. As far as I know no one has ever died from a terminal lack of entertainment saturation. The benefit of this practice is that gradually your brain will get less used to constantly having some low-quality information to chew on and will thus be better prepared to sustain focus on difficult tasks when you eventually find time in your schedule for deep work.

Of course it's going to be easier to conquer addiction if you break ties with your drug dealer. With that in mind Newport recommends *quitting social media*. Honest reflection will no doubt lead most people to realize that very little value is added to their lives by their online presence. It *is* useful to have a website, of course, and modest interaction with peers or a fanbase can be important (though Donald Knuth and science fiction writer Neal Stephenson get along just fine without these measures.)

Still. Each minute invested on Facebook tends to be a minute spent with very low return. I *do* use Facebook, and I suspect that I get more from it than most because I have a specific way of interacting with everyone's favorite social media platform. First and most importantly I spend little time on it. When I do post status updates they're usually thoughtful micro-essays or excerpts from this book. Second, I've always been pretty rigorous in trimming down my list of friends. Other than family I only maintain contact with people who have proven their ability to engage in honest, thoughtful conversation. As a result I've gotten quite a bit of free editing of my writing and useful critiques of my ideas, such that I'm reasonably confident that Facebook has been a net positive for me.

This dovetails nicely with Newports admonition to adopt a *craftsman approach* to tool selection. A craftsman, he argues, only uses tools which have substantially more advantages than disadvantages. A novice carpenter might hoard every tool he comes across because he lacks the knowledge required for nuanced evaluation. A master, however, gets far more done with a more careful selection of useful tools.

I don't use Twitter or Instagram because I've identified no upside to them. But thanks to my careful Facebook habits, I have been able to turn a source of pointless distraction into a source of insight; whole essays have been rewritten and made better because some friend of mine has spotted an error, made an interesting connection that hadn't occurred to me, or otherwise critiqued my work for free.

Lastly, we are to *drain the shallows* by reducing or eliminating the meetings, emails, messages, and other low-value tasks which shatter the work day and prevents focused depth. Newport elucidates this rule through the compelling example of 37signals, a technology company whose CEO took the then-radical step of reducing the workweek from five 8-hour days to four. Total output was unchanged because everyone was compelled to focus solely on the most important tasks. Seeing how well this worked 37signals enacted a policy of taking the *entire month of June (!)* off so that employees could work on big, company-changing ideas. These ideas were then fleshed out and presented at a 'pitch day' to the whole company. As of 2016 -- the year *Deep Work* was published -- this practice has led to two big new projects being actively developed.

***

37

Books like *Deep Work* are more important than their deceptive simplicity would imply. There are many works whose value derives from the fact that they challenge previously unshakeable assumptions and raise profound new questions. A good example is Julian Jaynes's *The Origins of Consciousness in the Breakdown of the Bicameral Mind*. In it he draws on linguistic analysis, textual exegesis, art, and myriad other disciplines to argue that peoples such as the ancient Greeks simply weren't conscious in the same way modern humans are. The result is difficult to dismiss, despite how crazy it might sound upfront.

There are also many works whose value derives from the fact that they expand areas of knowledge which you hadn't even realized you were glossing over. I didn't know how little I knew about Pre-Columbian American Indians before I read Charles C. Mann's *1491*. Though I had cursory knowledge of the Incas, the Toltecs, the Mayans, the Iroquois, and so on, reading an extended treatment of their respective societies opened my eyes to a richness and diversity I hadn't been aware of.

But there are many valuable works which don't do anything more than tell you something you already mostly knew in a way that makes the knowledge more resonant and actionable. In addition to *Deep Work* another favorite example is Josh Waitzkin's remarkable *The Art of Learning*. A brief summary of its thesis is 'you should spend a lot of time mastering the fundamentals of a field'.

I doubt anyone will find that revelatory. And yet I have re-read *The Art of Learning* maybe a dozen times. It isn't the message per se that I love, but the author's lucid and accessible style together with illustrations from his life as a star in competitive chess and martial arts. Seeing the astonishing results obtained by a person who so totally embodies his own simple philosophy inspires me to try to do the same.

This is worth bearing in mind from the perspective of both a potential writer of and reader of books. It's not always about the message. If I were to write a book that boils down to 'exercise is good and you should be doing it', it might not seem worth reading. But if I were to couch this bromide in stories about how a grandmother used exercise to reclaim the ability to play with her grandchildren, or built a philosophical justification for exercise by relating it to various historical warrior traditions, many people who already endorse the basic message might be compelled to act on it more consistently.

Similarly, *Deep Work* and Newport's other essays are not a towering intellectual edifice that inspires fear and awe, but a carefully built retaining wall that keeps the rain from eroding a hillside; not a white-hot beacon of truth, but a lantern showing a staircase that you overlooked in your haste.

Newport's success seems to come from the ruthless application of a handful of basic techniques, all of which I understand (but don't practice) just as well as he does.

He belongs to a different, in some ways even rarer class of thinkers that tells you things you already knew, but in a way that makes it all completely obvious and with clear, concise instructions in place for how to better implement knowledge.

I call people like this 'ultrapraxists', and it's to them that we now turn.

Chapter 4
The Ultrapraxists

Thanks to an invite from a good friend I was able to participate in a weekend session of Sebastian Marshall's 'ultraworking pentathlon' early in 2017.

The pentathlon consisted of five 'cycles', with each cycle broken into two parts: an uninterrupted 30-minute work period followed by a 10 minute break. Before each cycle you ask yourself the following questions:

1. What do I plan on accomplishing?
2. How will I begin?
3. What hazards are present?
4. What are my energy and morale like?

And after each cycle you ask yourself these questions:

1. Did I accomplish my goal?
2. Were there any hazards present?
3. How will I improve for my next cycle?
4. What are my energy and morale like?

Additionally, at the beginning of a pentathlon you ask yourself this set of questions just once:

1. What's my first priority today?
2. Why is this important for me?

3. How will I know when I've finished?

4. Any dangers present (procrastination etc.)?

5. Estimated number of cycles required?

6. Is my goal concrete or subjective?

And of course when you finish you debrief with this list of questions:

1. What did I get done this session?

2. How does this compare to my normal output?

3. Where did I consistently get bogged down? Is this part of a pattern?

4. What big improvement can I make in future cycles?

So each individual cycle is bracketed with before and after questions, and the whole macro-structure is bracketed with before and after questions. At first glance this may look tedious and distracting, but once you get used to it it only requires a few seconds.

Though this is just an adaptation of the familiar Pomodoro method, the questions form a metacognitive framework which confers several advantages:

First, asking questions like 'why is this important to me' is a great way to orient towards a task. Once I get focused it's often not difficult to stay motivated hour-to-hour, but it can be very difficult to stay motivated day-to-day. Reminding myself of why I've chosen to work on a project at the start of each session helps to mitigate this problem.

Second, it encourages frequent reflection on the learning process and facilitates rapid iteration of new techniques, preserving those that work and discarding those that don't. It's easy to have a great idea for an improvement in your work process but to then to get so absorbed in actually working that you either forget to implement the idea or you implement it but don't notice whether it actually works.

These are non-trivial improvements. In chapter 7 I advanced the idea that the mind can be thought of as a structure with attention and motivation flowing through it like liquids, with mantras, visualization, and a host of other 'self-improvement' techniques being akin to engineering depressions in this structure towards which those liquids flow. Simply wanting to form a habit often isn't enough, for example, so building a mantra stack around the habit is like putting a bowling ball on a trampoline: everything is more likely to drift toward the new default behavior. Ultraworking is a scaffold making this process quicker and more efficient. Good ideas can be tested and their results measured in just a few cycles while you simultaneously probe for larger regularities in your output and get actual work done. It's great!

The development of the ultraworking pentathlon places Sebastian Marshall squarely in the company of thinkers like Scott Young and Cal Newport (hereafter abbreviated as 'MYN et al.'), whose stratospheric achievement is built on the consistent application of simple, pretty-obvious-in-retrospect techniques. This contrasts with figures like Srinivasa Ramanujan, who was one of the most prodigious mathematicians to have ever lived.

By his own account Ramanujan would dream of Hindu Gods and Goddesses while complex mathematics unfolded before his eyes. Decades after his untimely death people are still finding uses for the theorems in his legendary notebooks.

What can *I* learn from a mind like that? Not much. But I can learn a ton from MYN et al. While these guys are very smart, I'm pretty sure Gods aren't downloading math into their brains while they sleep. Yet they still manage to write books, run businesses, prove new theorems, have kids, and stay in shape.

As valuable as the Ramanujans of the world are, MYN et al. might be even more valuable. Their bread and butter consists of admonitions like:

1) 'Block off as much time as possible to work on hard tasks because switching tasks is distracting.'

2) 'Summarize concepts in your own words because then you'll remember them better.'

3) 'Use Pomodoros, but ask yourself questions before and after so that you'll stay on track.'

4) etc...

Anyone smart enough to read is smart enough to do that. This means that while Ramanujan can do mathematics that twenty other people on Earth can even understand, MYN et al. can raise the average productivity of tens of thousands of people, maybe by orders of magnitude in extreme cases. I'm not positive that makes their net positive impact bigger than Ramanujan's, but I wouldn't be surprised if it were.

Any group of thinkers that important should have a name, and here's my proposal: The Ultrapraxists. 'Praxis' comes from Latin and refers to 'action' or 'practice' (think: orthopraxy). I kicked around a few different ideas for this title, but since Sebastian Marshall calls his technique 'ultraworking' and Scott Young just published a book on 'ultralearning' I settled on 'ultrapraxist'.

Read ultrapraxy, learn from it, and be the most productive possible version of yourself.

Chapter 5
A Taxonomy of Gnoses

Anyone who was studied a difficult technical subject like mathematics has surely had the following experience:

You wake up at 5:30 in the morning, determined to go over the tricky set theory proofs which looked like hieroglyphics to you the day before. There's a test over the material later in the week and, with an already packed schedule, it's imperative that you master this as quickly as possible.

Coffee brewed, you crack open the textbook and begin to go over the proofs. As usual it takes a quarter of an hour for the caffeine and the context to saturate your brain. By the time the first rays of morning lance through the twilight you've settled into time-worn scholarly rhythms.

But you're rediscovering, to your consternation, that studying math rarely produces insights in linear time. After days of fruitless concentration insight could drop from the sky like a nuclear bomb, and there's no guarantee that two concepts of roughly-equivalent difficulty will require a roughly-equivalent amount of time to grasp. Worse, there doesn't even seem to be a clear process you can fall back on to force understanding. At least with history you can just slow down, take copious notes, and be reasonably confident that the bigger picture will fade into view.

Not so with set theory. You've already come to a step which you simply cannot make sense out of. With your intuitions spinning their tires in the mud of a topic they didn't evolve to handle, you post a question to math.stackexchange and try desperately to understand the replies. Alas, even several rounds of follow-up questions don't resolve the problem.

Now you're just sort of…staring at the proof, chanting it to yourself like a Litany Against Ignorance. You keep going back to the start, working through the first couple of steps that make sense, re-reading the preceding section for clues, reading ahead a little bit for yet more clues, and so on. Perhaps you try stackexchange again, or watch related videos on Youtube.

After ninety minutes of this you take a break and reflect back on the morning's work. Not only do you not understand the set theory proofs, you're not even sure what to type into Google to find the next step. If a friend were to ask you point blank what you've been doing, you'd struggle to formulate a reply.

And yet…some of the words *do* seem less arcane, and the structure of the proof feels more familiar somehow, like a building you pass on your way to work everyday but have never really stopped to look at. You have this nagging feeling that something-like-insight is hovering just out of your mind's peripheral vision. You finish this study session with a vague, indefinable sense that progress *has* been made.

I call this frustrating state 'semignosis'[19], and have spent a lot of time in it over the course of the STEMpunk Project. Once I had this term I realized there were a lot of interesting ideas I could generate by attaching different prefixes to 'gnosis', and thus I developed the following taxonomy:

- Agnosis, n. — Simply not knowing something.
- Semignosis, n. — The state described above, where the seeds of future gnosis are being sown but there is no current, specifiable increase in knowledge.

---

[19] I realize I'm mixing Greek and Latin here.

- Infragnosis, n. — knowledge which you didn't know you had; the experience of being asked a random question and surprising yourself by giving an impromptu ten-minute lecture in reply.

- Gnosis, n. — Knowing something, be it a procedure or a fact.

- Misgnosis, n. — 'Knowing' something which turns out not to be true.

- Supergnosis, n. — Suddenly grokking a concept, i.e. having an insight. Comes in a 'local' flavor (having an insight new to you) or a 'global' flavor (having an insight no one has ever had before).

If we wanted to we could keep extending this analysis:

- Misinfragnosis, n. — Knowledge you don't gnow you had, but which (alas) ends up being untrue.

- Gnostic phantom, n. — A false shape which jumps out at you because of the way an argument is framed or pieces are arranged; the mental equivalent of a Kanisza figure[20].

- Saturated gnosis, n. — 'Common knowledge'

- Saturated infragnosis, n. — 'Common sense', or knowledge everyone has but probably doesn't think about consciously unless asked to do so.

This is mostly just for fun. We already have a word for 'insight' so the word 'supergnosis' is superfluous. I doubt any of these terms will be used outside of this chapter.

But I think the term 'semignosis' is genuinely important. It captures a real state through which we must pass in our efforts to learn, and a very frustrating one at that. Having the term potentially allows us to do three things:

---

[20]   https://www.princeton.edu/~freshman/kanizsa.html

1. We can recognize the state as real and necessary, perhaps alleviating some of the distress felt while occupying it.

2. We can begin to classify fields by the amount of time a student of average intelligence must spend in semignosis.

3. We can start to think more clearly about how to approach and navigate this state.

While I hope to develop more sophisticated strategies for shortening the amount of time spent in semignostic states, as of this writing I don't have much advice other than: take heart, because we've all been there. If you persist understanding will eventually come.

Chapter 6
Entity Theory and Identity Theory

If I told you that there was a factor exerting a profound effect on your likelihood of success in learning which had nothing to do with intelligence, access to resources, prior knowledge, or training, would you be interested in knowing about it?

I thought so.

Imagine that we're in an advanced high school math class and we've just met two students: Rebecca and Genevieve. Both are clearly intelligent and both are passionately in love with mathematics. Rebecca has known she was a little special for as far back as she can remember. Hardly a week has passed without her having gotten the highest score in one of her classes, she's been a regular at the regional geography and spelling bees, and received one of the highest SAT scores in the county.

Rebecca has always approached mathematics like a child climbing through the basement and rafters of an abandoned building that's become a secret refuge. She was in fourth grade when she first pulled Euclid's *Elements* from her aunt's bookshelf and began to slowly turn its pages. The adults around her had more or less concluded that she was a genius on the spot, and told her so with alacrity. For a shy, bright girl like her, receiving so much positive attention had been wonderful.

Even that far back she had struggled less with mathematics than her peers. Her teachers and parents all thought this came down to talent, so she supposed that it must be true. Sometimes she felt sorry for those whose innate grasp of theorems, proofs, and equations just couldn't match her own, though of course she never voiced this pity. It was like not being able to see or smell -- she just couldn't imagine how fuliginous the world would be without the clarity born of mathematical understanding. It wasn't fair that she excelled with only 15% of the effort required by everyone else, but there was nothing to be done about it.

She was a natural, after all.

Genevieve has always been intelligent but has never had the slightest problem rolling up her sleeves when required. Because her mother had worked two jobs while getting a nursing degree Genevieve had never lacked a ready example of a strong work ethic. She doesn't know whether she inherited or learned her own grit from her mother, but she applied it to school and had been recognized as a star pupil by the time she was in fourth grade.

She loves nothing half so well as mathematics -- there is a slow thrill that comes when she finally grasps a new concept. She assumes it must be what a master stonemason would've felt when the last stone of a cathedral were put into place. After days of measurement, building, levelling, carving, scaffolding, lifting, suddenly...it clicks, and some new phenomenon would become explicable to her.

Genevieve has routinely been placed in advanced math classes, and she has always had a vague sense that she must study a bit harder than some of the other children in those classes. This doesn't matter to her at all -- the price of a little more work for so much understanding seems more than reasonable. Her mother has always given her mute praise for her grades, preferring instead to emphasize the value of the *work* involved in their attainment. She has no idea why her peers are averse to effort. It seemed a shame that so many things would be closed to them because they couldn't be bothered to try, but there was nothing to be done about.

She loves the learning process, after all.

***

In the late 1980's Carol Dweck began exploring terrain which would ignite decades of productive psychological research into how motivation affects performance. Her early work[21] pinpointed two motivational styles, one adaptive and one maladaptive. Individuals exhibiting the adaptive *mastery* orientation tended to not only persist in the face of difficulties and setbacks, but to actively seek out new challenges. They were far more interested in pushing their abilities than in resting on past achievements.

This was less the case for individuals exhibiting the maladaptive *helpless* orientation. These people tended to be more brittle, and to avoid tasks which might demonstrate that their mastery of a subject wasn't as high as everyone had thought it was. These responses emerge from the kinds of goals the individuals had. A *performance goal* is one aimed at getting praise for a job well done while a *mastery goal* is one aimed at improvement. These goals become a framework driving a person's evaluation of themselves, their skills, and the things that happen to them. Because a person with a performance goal really cares more about how their abilities raise or lower their standing in the eyes of other people they are prone to the maladaptive pattern of helplessness. Failures are not seen as a chance to grow but as a net loss in esteem. This is less of a concern for a person with a mastery goal because they care about getting better. Mistakes are a fee paid for achievement, and no one rises without making plenty of them.

Pulling on this thread led Dweck and her colleagues to a still bigger insight: the reason that some people have performance goals and others have mastery goals derives from deeper, implicit theories of intelligence and ability. These implicit theories come in the now-famous 'entity' and 'incremental' flavors.

An entity theorist views intelligence as a fixed entity which naturally leads to performance goals that document the scope of their immutable talent. With this orientation failures are evidence that the limits of an ability have been reached; as there is little hope for improvement, failures are so disheartening that the entity theorist

---

[21]   https://mathedseminar.pbworks.com/f/Dweck+%26+Leggett+(1988)+A+soci al-cognitive+approach+to+motivation+and+personality.pdf

may go to great lengths to avoid them altogether. An incremental theorist sees intelligence as a flexible, malleable suite of abilities which can be improved with the right approach and sufficient effort. Incremental theorists don't like failures -- I doubt anyone does -- but they don't see failures in the same catastrophic terms as entity theorists do.

No doubt it's obvious that in the above vignette Rebecca is an entity theorist and Genevieve is an incremental theorist. Both girls are highly intelligent and very accomplished, but they each have deeply-held beliefs which determine their approach to learning. Which do you think is more likely to rebound from a serious setback? Which do you think is more likely to deliberately seek out difficult new challenges?

Put another way: if we know about the distinction between entity and incremental theories and we know which theory a given person holds, what can we predict about them?

A number of studies[22] indicate that learning theories have profound cognitive, affective, and behavioral consequences. Children with performance goals and children with learning goals use different rules for interpreting failure and exertion. In the context of a performance goal both failures and effort are indicators of low ability. If you have to work hard and still don't succeed, then you must not be very good at whatever you're doing. But in the context of a learning goal this isn't the case. Hard work is simply viewed as a mechanism for accessing stores of talent, and failures as evidence that more effort will be required. Children with learning goals are more likely to grow bored with tasks that are too easy, and may even value mastery of a difficult skill precisely *because* it's difficult. In several studies they have been observed spontaneously issuing 'battle cries' and promises of eventual success.

---

[22]   Unfortunately I was only able to track down a limited number of these studies. Unless I've cited a specific paper you should assume any information comes from Dweck and Leggett's 1988 'A Social-Cognitive Approach to Motivation and Personality'.

Feelings of shame and embarrassment often accompany failure when one holds a performance goal. Self esteem is deeply entangled with the evaluations of other people, and these evaluations are highest when one can be observed succeeding with virtually no effort at all. This obviously creates an incentive for avoiding true tests of ability and makes one more likely to pretend not to care about a task if it looks like failure is possible.

A learning goal makes one far more likely to persist in a difficult task. In addition to the fact that people with learning goals are more intrinsically motivated by hard work they may be spending less energy preemptively coming up with excuses for their failure and fretting over the possibility of having their esteem lowered in the eyes of their peers. Whatever the case may be all the evidence points to their having a much healthier relationship with the pursuit of excellence, which invariably produces large amounts of failure and adversity that must be overcome.

Now that we have a greater understanding of how much our success is affected by our implicit theories of learning, the obvious next question is: what can we do about it?

I know for a fact that it's possible to make the transition from entity to incremental theorist because I've done it myself. Once I learned of the two implicit learning theories I began to notice behavioral patterns which indicated that I was avoiding new challenges for fear that my natural talents wouldn't be enough to make success extremely likely. Because I was a good guitarist I never tried to sing; because I was good at philosophy and science I eschewed math, in which I was weak; because I could bench press 280 lbs. in high school I never deadlifted because I was terrible at it.

This is a kind of inversion of the popular idea that 'the perfect is the enemy of the good', a sentiment which is usually interpreted to mean that you'll never finish a task if you insist on its being absolutely flawless. In my case, however, my own achievements were cutting off the possibility of achieving even more; some people rest on their laurels, and others are weigh down by them.

For me just noticing the problem was enough to begin to fix it. But I had also been keeping reflective journals and striving to better myself for many years at that point. If you're less practiced I would suggest utilizing some of the techniques I discussed in an earlier chapter. You might develop a mantra stack, a set of aspirations, or some visualization exercises around interpreting failures as a chance to grow instead of evidence that you aren't good enough. If your entity theory is very deeply ingrained you might consider devoting some time to a hobby or skill at which you are terrible. Take a dance class if you're a physically awkward mathematician, or a math class if you're lithe and graceful. I've noticed a lot of my introverted nerd friends getting into improvisational comedy recently.

The point here isn't so much to become good at the skill, though obviously that's a bonus. It's to force yourself to do something in which you have no background and no natural advantages. You have to become more comfortable staring down the possibility of failure. Once you've done that you can import this ability to fields where you *do* have an advantage, in the hopes that you'll be less afraid to begin climbing from whatever plateau you've been on.

STEMpunk

Chapter 7
Motivation and Project Structure

I had many reasons for wanting to undertake the STEMpunk Project: I love computers and programming; I read an almost unhealthy amount of science fiction, to the exclusion of nearly every other kind of fiction; the idea of investing in tech startups is appealing, and I think I might be good at it; the world still has a dire shortage of people doing long-term, sensible analyses of emerging technologies, and perhaps I can help with some small part of that.

Plus, I've been fascinated by technology as far back as I can remember, but for various reasons have failed to nurture or explore that fascination.

Last year I decided to change that.

Thinking Inside the (Black) Box.

Alfred North Whitehead once said that '[c]ivilization advances by extending the number of important operations which we can perform without thinking about them.' This resonates with my own view of civilization as the proliferation of black boxes, i.e. things whose internal workings are either unknown or sealed away and not encountered directly in the normal course of living.

In the course of debating this notion it was pointed out to me that a black box can also be a process one understands but never considers. A programmer, for example, might have a theoretical understanding of the algorithms for finding square roots but never think about those algorithms when using them in their code.

Pondering this led me to make the following distinctions:

- Glass box -- the internal components are transparent and can be manipulated mentally or manually, disassembled and reassembled, repaired and upgraded at will. Glass boxes represent a professional or near-professional level of understanding.

- Gray box -- the internal components are grasped abstractly. You could have a reasonably detailed conversation with a person for whom transistors were a glass box, and perhaps explain in broad terms how transistors work, but couldn't repair one or design an improved version.

- Black box -- components are almost entirely mysterious. Perhaps you could give a vague account of their functioning using vocabulary you barely understand, but you almost certainly couldn't diagnose a black box failure or take one apart with any confidence that you could reassemble it.

For additional clarity I would add the following distinctions between 'primitives' and 'pseudo-primitives':

- Primitive -- the simplest conceptual unit or operation of a given domain. The primitive operations of basic arithmetic are addition and subtraction.

- Pseudo-primitive -- composite operations which are treated as primitives. Multiplication is technically just repeated addition (i.e. 3 x 5 is just 3 + 3 + 3 + 3 + 3) but most of us think of it as being a primitive in its own right.

For a programmer who has no idea how square roots are calculated the relevant algorithm is a black box. If that programmer comes to vaguely understand the process then the algorithm is a gray box. When the programmer eventually understands the algorithm in great detail it has become a glass box, and years later when she uses it without thinking about it at all it is a pseudo-primitive.

If you use a glass box without considering its internal components then it would be best to describe it as a 'pseudo-primitive', not a 'black box'.

Let's extend this out with another example: what is a refrigerator? Well, it's a device that keeps food cold. I know that it doesn't work if I leave the door open, which implies that some amount of sealing is required. I don't know what freon is or what it does, but I have heard it mentioned in connection with air conditioners and other cooling apparatuses, so I assume it is involved somehow. At my level of understanding refrigerators are a clear example of a black box.

Luckily an entire segment of the economy exists to manufacture, distribute, repair, and improve upon refrigeration technologies, and they get along perfectly well without me. For these people, refrigerators are glass boxes. Thanks to them I can cheerfully write computer code without having to also invent refrigeration, and when I get hungry I can just open the refrigerator, pull something out, and eat it without having to go hunting.

Now let's return to the notion that civilization is the proliferation of black boxes. For the most part this is a good thing, and my ignorance is usually harmless. Still, I don't think it's good to have too many things I rely on every day be mysterious. As a man with a growing degree of responsibility I should probably have some idea of how to do basic car repairs, what an electrical panel is and the rudiments of how to wire one, what a computer is and how to build one, etc.

So the STEMpunk Project was motivated in part by a sense of duty: I want to move more things from the 'black box' category to the 'gray/glass box' and 'pseudo-primitive' categories so that I can be a more effective man. But besides that, as I grow older I find myself increasingly fascinated by how awe-inspiringly *incredible* this stuff is.

How many eons did man spend cowering in fear under rock ledges because some vicious lightning storm or forest fire was raging just beyond his shelter? How many gods were invented and placated because man not only didn't know what he was looking at, but hadn't yet even conceived of a general method for understanding what he was looking at?

These days, however, lightning is channeled through hidden conduits in my walls so that I can keep my living room a comfortable 75 degrees year round, and I use fire to propel a metal cage sitting on four inflated rubber donuts down a ribbon of asphalt at twice the top speed of a horse. These miracles are called 'electricity' and 'driving', and they're so common as to be boring.

To borrow a technical scientific phrase: that is *awesome*.

Not Just About the Technology

While the STEMpunk Project was about cultivating a richer set of models of various technical systems, on a deeper level it was about developing two macro-abilities which will allow me to begin playing at the level of the people I most admire:

1) Building the strength of focus to make rapid progress and produce large quantities of value.

2) Conceiving of, planning, and executing large-scale learning projects with many degrees of uncertainty.

I managed to do that, and this book will help you to do that as well.

Issues in Large-Scale Planning

The project was originally divided into Computing, Electronics, Mechanics, and Robotics modules, each of which was subdivided into three or four *stages*, and each of which had the following cadence: first, there was an applied component centered primarily on toy projects like building model engines. This was then followed by a theoretical component that involved reading books and watching lectures. Finally came a more serious set of applied projects, like wiring an electrical panel or rebuilding a lawn mower engine.

In trying to decide how best to proceed I ran into some problems that weren't as salient in similar endeavors like Scott Young's MIT Challenge[23]. To start with I had no idea in what order I should learn various concepts or perform smaller hands-on projects. While I tried reaching out to a number of engineering professors and experts for advice, the only response I ever received was 'I'm sorry, how do I know you?'

Further, I wanted to make sure that I didn't spend all my time simply reading theory. A major goal of the STEMpunk Project was getting better at making and doing stuff. While this didn't work out the way I'd hoped it would, it was a significant factor in the early planning stages.

How should one go about learning a complex discipline with both dense theoretical aspects and hands-in-the-dirt applied aspects? The solution I eventually settled on was iterating between theory and practice in a specific way. To get my bearings in mechanics, for example, I wanted to begin by spending a few weeks playing with model engines to help shape my intuitions about how mechanical systems work. Then I wanted to immerse myself in mechanical engineering by watching lectures and books, refining and deepening the understanding developed previously. With that knowledge I then wanted to try to work with actual hardware like a busted motorcycle engine.

This approximates the default strategy used by many as they go about learning mechanics on their own. As children they are given erector sets or model rockets, and pass many happy afternoons getting various components to fit together properly. This stage may last throughout their high school years, before they eventually enter into an auto repair trade school. After spending a while mastering the theory they begin a career which allows them to further their life-long interests by working as a professional repairman or technician.

My plans were made with this template in mind.

---

23   https://www.scotthyoung.com/blog/myprojects/mit-challenge-2/

Another major problem was that the lack of guidance meant a lot of uncertainty over the life of the project. How, after all, is a novice supposed to calculate the length of time required to learn basic electrical theory if he has no frame of reference?

I coped by deliberately marking out where the uncertain places were and trying to leave myself plenty of time to complete them. I only had a vague idea, for example, of how the robotics portion was going to unfold, and in particular how long it would take me to learn whatever programming is involved.

Another thing I might have done was plan out a few different alternatives for each module, perhaps with rankings like 'easy', 'moderate', and 'difficult'. Or I could've set the modules up with branches which forked depending on whether or not I'd made a certain amount of progress, so that if I had managed to do *A* then I would do *B*, and if not then instead I would do *C*.

In the end I decided against this approach because I have a proclivity towards getting too caught up in the planning stage. I can't recommend that everyone follow my lead, but it made more sense for me to pick an arbitrary date (March 1st) and just start the damn thing, even though that meant I wound up biting off more than I could chew.

***

In summary I dealt with the following three problems:

1. Ignorance with regards to the optimal learning order;
2. The need to balance theory with practice;
3. The inherent uncertainty of a beginner trying to allot a reasonable amount of time to accomplish a big goal.

In the following three ways:

1. Iterate between theory and practice;
2. Bias the modules toward applied instead of theoretical work;
3. Leave large margins in my time estimates;

Before I go through the process of detailing all the ways in which I deviated from my original outline, I want to point out how important it is at least *try* to plan when beginning a project of any magnitude. Vague slogans and unarticulated ambitions might be enough to get started on a large project, but they aren't enough to see it through to the end. Actually finishing, or even making enough progress to not feel bad about the time invested, requires careful and consistent forethought.

This is true even when this forethought later proves inadequate.

How the STEMpunk Project was *Supposed* to Unfold

Here is the outline with which I began the project[24]:

COMPUTING[25] (Estimated time: 10 WEEKS)

Stage I: Spend two hours a day or so reading books about building computers and putting a parts list together. Run the list by more technically inclined friends and then, if money isn't tight, order the parts.

I reasoned that even if I wasn't able to actually build the computer until later in the year the process of researching components and how they interrelate would be an invaluable learning experience.

Stage II: Read as much of 'The Elements of Computing Systems' as possible, doing the programming exercises as time allowed.

---

[24] Elsewhere in the book I include in-text and footnote citations, but in this chapter there were so many I decided to leave them at: https://rulerstothesky. com/2016/03/10/the-stempunk-project-goals-and-how-to-achieve-them/   If you're interested in the kits and books I discuss, you'll find more information at this link.

[25] Several people took issue with my use of the term 'Computing'. What I mean is just 'anything to do with computers, including things like building computers.' This isn't the standard usage, but other terms like 'Computer Science' are just as problematic.

Stage III: Allocate two hours a day to working through the CompTIA A+ book on basic PC troubleshooting and repair. Get a CompTIA certification if it seems worth having. Repeat the process with the CompTIA Network+ and Security+ books.

ELECTRONICS (Estimated time: 8 WEEKS)

Stage I: Swallow my pride enough to play with some kid's toys[26]. The tentative list included the 'SparkFun Inventor's Kit', around 5 or so soldering projects from the 'Elenco Practical Soldering Project Kit', a '200-in-1 electronics project kit' (though I never committed to doing all 200), the SparkFUN Photon kit, the SparkFUN Car Diagnostics Kit, the SparkFUN LabVIEW kit, and the SparkFUN Raspberry PI starter kit[27].

Stage II: Begin the theory stage by reading books, completing tutorials (like the one from sparkfun.com or the one from electronic-tutorials.ws), and taking classes like 'Circuits and Electronics', 'Introduction to Electronics Signals and Measurement', 'Practical Electronics', 'Advanced Circuit Techniques', 'Power Electronics', and 'Electrical Machines'[28].

Stage III: Make an inventory of all the electrical devices and systems in my house. Go through them and see how much my new-found knowledge allows me to understand, cataloging the remaining gaps. I wanted to fill those gaps by arranging to have a contractor/electrician come to my house and spend half a day explaining it all to me.

---

[26] I recommend this. Science and engineering kits aimed at children are obviously simple, but they're not stupid. An adult with no working knowledge of the field could absolutely benefit from play with them.

[27] Any of these can be found with a quick search of Amazon or Google.

[28] These and other classes referenced in this section are offered through MIT's excellent Open CourseWare initiative. Find links for everything at: https://rulerstothesky.com/2016/03/10/the-stempunk-project-goals-and-how-to-achieve-them/

Stage IV: Reach out to an electrician friend and offer to do some free work for him in exchange for a fast-paced apprenticeship lasting a couple of weeks.

MECHANICS (Estimated Time: 6 WEEKS)

Stage I: Begin with kid's toys like a 16-project Erector set, a model v8 Engine Kit, a model jet engine, models of Da Vinci Clocks and Da Vinci catapults, a stirling external combustion engine, an interactive 'how cars work' children's book, and perhaps others.

Stage II: Move on to theory, by reading books like 'Basics of Mechanical Engineering', 'Basic Machines and How They Work', '1800 Mechanical Movements, Devices, and Appliances', '507 Mechanical Movements', 'How Cars Work', and 'How Machines Work'. Take some classes like 'Engineering Mechanics I', 'Engineering Mechanics II', 'How and Why Machines Work', 'Internal Combustion Engines', and maybe even 'Elements of Mechanical Design'.

Stage III: Make an inventory of all the electrical devices and systems in my house. Go through them and see how much my newfound knowledge allows me to understand, cataloging the remaining gaps. Either make a plan to fill those gaps or arrange to have a contractor/electrician come to my house and spend half a day explaining it all to me.

Stage IV: Proceed through a series of real-life disassemble/repair/reassemble projects of escalating complexity. Though I never had a detailed plan, I wanted to progress along the lines of coffee maker, water pump, weed eater motor, and cheap old motorcycle.

ROBOTICS (~10 WEEKS)

I was actually most excited about this module, after computing. The plan was to use what I'd learned in electronics, computing, mechanics, and programming to do some basic home automation. I had this vision of myself walking through my living room and casually throwing out commands in a few different foreign languages to my refrigerator, the blender, little robot arms holding up six computer monitors bolted to my custom-built desktop computer, etc.

Stage I: I needed to keep this part lean because stage three would involve a heavy software component with a steep learning curve[29]. I planned to do a few projects like the Electronictechcrafts 14-in-1 solar robot kit, the Monoprice Robot Kit, and maybe the SparkFUN RedBot kit to get oriented.

Stage II: Take some classes like 'Introduction to Robotics', 'Lego Robotics', 'Mechatronics', and 'Design of Electromechanical Robotic Systems'. Perhaps read 'Robot Building for Beginners' and look at the Sparkfun robotics tutorials.

Stage III: I never planned this out in any detail. I had ideas for basic home automation but no way of calibrating the difficulty of getting them done. My hope was that by the end of stages I and II I would know enough to be able to make a more sophisticated plan.

'No plan survives contact with the enemy', a quote attributed to numerous sources, adequately captures the fact that no matter how thorough our attempts at planning we all end up grappling with chaos in the end. Let's turn now to a discussion of how well my plan held up as the STEMpunk Project unfolded.

---

[29] One beta reader pointed out that robotics needn't necessarily be software intensive. I trust his expertise, but I didn't know that during the planning stages.

Chapter 8
Contact With the Enemy

It's impossible to know what you don't know in advance. I made the best assumptions I could and did the best research possible, but there wound up being a rather large chasm between 'STEMpunk theory' and 'STEMpunk practice'. Below I discuss this chasm and the lessons I learned from it.

Computing

Because I'm fascinated by computers I started the project with the Computing module, hoping to build enough momentum to carry me through the rest of the way. I read three books on PC construction: 'Build Your Own PC' by Mark Chambers, 'Building the Perfect PC' by Robert and Barbara Thompson, and 'Building Extreme PCs' by Ben Hardwidge. Any of them will serve you well if you're thinking about building a system of your own.

Budgeting issues prevented me from actually building the desktop I designed. I had a vague idea of how much a system would cost, and when I made the initial plans I had enough money to buy all the required components. As the year progressed, however, I simultaneously hit a rough patch and paid taxes, so my savings had to be tapped to handle basic expenses. I still haven't built my desktop, though I still have the parts list; perhaps in a year or so I can move forward with construction.

The second stage of the Computing module was devoted to Noam Nisan and Shimon Schocken's outstanding book 'The Elements of Computing Systems', in which students build a virtual computer from NAND gates up, implementing RAM, assemblers, virtual machines, and everything else required for a computer to function.

The first stage took longer to complete than I anticipated, so the second stage had to be squeezed into less time to keep me on schedule. As a result I only did a fraction of the actual coding exercises involved. If you have enough time to do the programming then I can't recommend 'Elements' enough. You might also consider looking into William Stallings' 'Computer Organization and Architecture'[30], which is far more detailed and features study questions at the end of each chapter.

Electronics

Of all the modules, Electronics might've been the one which most closely followed the plan and involved the most hands-on work. I listed seven projects for *stage I* and ended up completing three of them[31]: the SparkFun Inventor's Kit, numerous exercises from the Elenco Electronics Playground 130, and the Elenco Practical Soldering Project Kit. For the final kit I bought a real-life soldering gun and solder and successfully wired a tiny speaker to play musical tones!

Well after I planned the theory module I ended up finding an excellent, near-comprehensive resource for electronics theory: a series of lectures given by Navy-trained electrician Joe Gryniak, available on Youtube. His jocular teaching style and vast store of practical knowledge mean that the attentive student will gain quite a lot from him. I wound up focusing on these lectures and Basic Electricity by the United States Navy for the entirety of *stage II*.

One of the first problems I ran into was trying to figure out how to read the schematics that accompany so many electronics projects. Here is an example of one:

---

[30] For what it's worth I'm told the Stallings book is one of the absolute best on the topic.

[31] Pictures of these kits are included in later chapters.

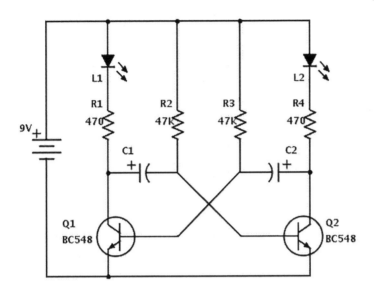

Both of the kits from *stage I* featured wiring diagrams which make reading the schematic unnecessary, but this step can't be skipped if you really want to understand the circuit and get as much as possible from the exercise. Plus, once the training wheels are off schematics become indispensable.

I started with learning the basic symbols for electrical components like resistors, capacitors, and so on. These three tutorials helped:

1. Sparkfun's 'How to Read a Schematic'.

2. An Instructable on How to Read a Circuit Diagram[32].

3. Make Magazine's tutorial[33] contains a nice summary near the end to which you might want to refer in the future.

But I still couldn't figure out how to translate the symbols and wire connections to an actual circuit. What I really needed was to see someone walk through a schematic while illustrating their process and building the physical device. Luckily some people

---

[32] http://www.instructables.com/id/HOW-TO-READ-CIRCUIT-DIAGRAMS/

[33] http://makezine.com/2011/01/25/reading-circuit-diagrams/

have done just that, and I've compiled a list of some of the better videos I found:

1. Collin Cunningham patiently lays out the basics of reading a schematic in his own oddball, funny way.[34]

2. Ben Heck's 'Principles of Schematics'[35] demonstrates schematic reading by building a touch plate LED circuit. Pay special attention to his method for laying out and keeping track of all those little components.

3. Youtuber Cold Redd's 'Reading Electronics Schematics'[36] is a very thorough explanation of interpreting and using schematics. Near the end of the video there are a number of close-up shots of the circuit he's built. Pause the video and make sure you can see where power is coming from and how it gets to the various pins on the Integrated Circuit. Hand draw the schematic for easy reference if needed.

4. Paul Wesley Lewis's 'How to read an Electronic Schematic'[37] walks you through a simple breadboard, carefully illustrating how each connection corresponds to a part of the schematic.

5. RimstarOrg's 'How to Read a Schematic'[38] video contains the simplest circuit and explains symbols for connections like a *chassis ground* which aren't contained in the other videos.

One of the difficulties in planning something like The STEMpunk Project is the simple fact that there often is just no way of telling in advance when some essential, basic skill is going to be required.

---

[34] https://www.youtube.com/watch?v=9cps7Q_lrX0

[35] https://www.youtube.com/watch?v=olRsMBVuSS4

[36] https://www.youtube.com/watch?v=DwCRXs3yzXo

[37] https://www.youtube.com/watch?v=MxRGXle1qPo

[38] https://www.youtube.com/watch?v=_HZ-EQ8Hc8E

But an ability to adapt to contingencies is useful in almost any project, so it's worth learning to do!

Mechanics

Like the Electronics module, the first two stages of the Mechanics module didn't deviate in any significant way from the plan. *Stage I* began with the construction of the Smithsonian's Motor-Works 4-cylinder model engine, the Smithsonian's Jet Works model jet engine, most of the models in the Meccano-Erector Super Construction Set, and the adorable but informative 'How Cars Work' by Nick Arnold, which was a cleverly-designed children's book that also contained very basic models of brakes, the steering column, and so on.

Stage II was devoted to the Navy's 'Basic Machines and How They Work', as well as sections of Singal, Singal, & Singal's 'Basics of Mechanical Engineering' In highsight the fact that I wasn't concerned with the mathematics of mechanical engineering meant that my time would probably have been better spent on Gardner Hiscox's '1800 Mechanical Movements, Devices, and Appliances', which I also bought but never got around to reading. These books were helpful and informative, but if I had it to do over I would skip them in favor of video-based materials. If you're less interested in the detailed mathematics involved in friction, shear, torque, and similar concepts you're better off building a qualitative understanding of mechanical systems, and that's best achieved by watching them function or be repaired.

Artificial Intelligence

The only major change made to the STEMpunk project occurred after life events forced me to reconsider the efficacy of the Robotics module.

Each of the modules was designed to expose me to theory while allocating plenty of time to actually tinker with physical devices. Robotics was included because it seemed like a natural extension of computing, electronics, and mechanics; but the more research

I did, the more I realized that acquiring a foundation in robotics involves a lot of programming[39].

There are good robotics kits out there, but most of them seemed unlikely to be as effective in cultivating intuitions as the model engines and electronics kits had been because they don't bear the same relationship to the actual physical systems which they represent. A toy engine may be wildly oversimplified but real engines also have cylinders, valves, a crankshaft, etc. As far as I can tell, however, code is the heart of robotics, and most of the kits I examined didn't factor that in.

So I reasoned that if I'm going to be programming anyway I may as well shift my focus to Artificial Intelligence instead of Robotics. AI is one of the fields I have considered exploring after the STEMpunk Project, and I have friends who are mathematicians, programmers, and philosophers with a keen interest in the issues involved.

Moreover, I'm twenty eight years old and must therefore give thought to the long-term stability of the people whose lives are bound up with mine. My family will be bigger by one when my daughter is born at the end of June 2017 and, besides that, with ebbing youth comes the fact that I have a finite number of years left in which to develop the skills I'm going to develop and make the contributions I'm going to make. Since AI is a serious interest of mine, I knew that spending the last leg of The STEMpunk Project working on it would seriously deepen my grasp of the field.

Finally, these days no one's job is really safe. The STEMpunk Project probably hasn't done that much to make me more employable, but a few months spent programming and playing with Machine Learning libraries -- especially if I continue on after the main project is finished -- probably will.

---

[39] Again this wound up being a faulty assumption. I have since been told there are quite a few robotics kits that involve little-to-no programming, but I was never able to find them!

With all that having been said, the AI module followed the template of the earlier modules. I began by completing Zed Shaw's excellent 'Learn Python the Hard Way', supplemented with his 'Command Line Crash Course', which I also recommend. Then I set my sights on 'Artificial Intelligence: A Modern Approach', a classic AI textbook by Stuart Russell and Peter Norvig widely considered to be among the seminal texts in the field.

I had been meaning to read AIMA ever since I developed an interest in artificial intelligence. For years it's been clear to me that AI is going to be one of the keystone technologies that define the future. As much as advances in transportation, manufacturing, communications, and war have opened enormous vistas of possibility and peril, the development of strong (read: approximately human-level) artificial intelligence could bring bigger changes *by far* because it would represent an improvement in the process which generates improvement. No matter how fast, cheap, or green our cars become they will never design an improved version of themselves -- unless they come loaded with software for that purpose.

As a result of this interest my knowledge of the field had been bimodal, with a cluster around set theory, computation, and mathematical logic and another around soaring philosophical questions such as the relationship between consciousness and intelligence or the thickets of machine ethics. But until AIMA I had never taken a close look at the area between these extremes, where actual engineers are busy tinkering with reinforcement learning algorithms, Markov Chain Monte Carlo methods, evolved hardware, software for voice, face, and object recognition, mechatronics, and other exotic djinn from the space of possible minds.

AIMA was an exhaustive tour of this middle terrain, complete with mathematical formalisms and pseudocode implementations. I didn't leave anywhere near enough time to do it proper justice, however, because I was anxious to begin writing the STEMpunk book. I'd give it at least six months, or a year if your background in math isn't very strong.

The final stage of the AI module is ongoing and open-ended. I have been programming in Python whenever I have the time, and I'm considering an AI nanodegree from Udacity or an equivalent sometime in the near future.

What Happened to the Final Stages?

You may have noticed that there is a glaring omission in the above: while my original plan had ample space devoted to rebuilding actual engines and wiring actual buildings, I haven't described *doing* any of that.

Well, that's because I didn't.

This is my only real regret with the STEMpunk Project. I was tremendously excited about getting my hands dirty in the final stages of each module, but when the time came to begin, each of them fell through.

Though in *stage III* of the Computing module I read the CompTIA A+ as planned I simply didn't have time to read the Security+ and Network+ books, let alone take any certification tests for them. There's no other way to put it: the fault here lies entirely with me for having made a plan that was hilariously overambitious.

The Electronics module was supposed to culminate in helping an electrician-friend wire a new building. He and I talked for several weeks about what would be involved, and I dutifully brushed up on Ohm's Law, wiring diagrams, and the details of subpanel installation. But the building took *much* longer than originally planned, which meant that wiring had to be delayed for weeks. By the time my friend got started, I had been forced to move on to the next module.

Something similar happened with the Mechanics module. Though my *stage IV* was originally slated to involve a series of hardware projects I caught wind of a friend who was planning to rebuild an old Porsche engine. I told him I would be happy to help because, while I had done some research on local scrap yards where I could get old machines to tinker with, my day job was consuming a larger-than-usual fraction of my time and I hadn't had a chance to follow through with acquiring anything to work on.

Alas, it ended up being the case that shipping the engine to Colorado would cost a prohibitive $900. And since I hadn't been actively working on a plan B, I faced the choice of either losing a few weeks while I explored alternatives or moving on.

I chose to move on to the final module. This is another place where I can't necessarily recommend everyone follow my lead. Ultimately I decided that there was too great a risk of the project losing momentum, and I would rather jettison a few stages than get bogged down in planning and never finish at all. If you're less prone to analysis paralysis, or if the module in question is extremely important to the overall success of the project, you might not have the same choice.

Should Goals be Heroic?

In hindsight it's clear that my goals simply were not achievable in the time I allotted. It would probably require two years to complete the original version of the project, with a full six months devoted to each module. As a matter of fact, if any of my readers decide they'd like to do their own STEMpunk Project I recommend they leave *at least* that much time.

But there's a bigger question here, concerning whether striving for something as ambitious as the STEMpunk Project or the MIT Challenge is stifling or motivating. Should you set your sights *that* high knowing there's a decent chance you'll fail, or try for something more modest and achievable?

The answer varies as a function of how you process failure[40]. Personally, I find lofty challenges force me to dig deep and try to actualize my highest potential, and that remains true even when I inevitably fall short. Like everyone else I have moments of self-doubt,

---

[40] Chapter 11 explores this issue in depth.

and these range from being merely unpleasant to being nearly crippling. But on the whole I'm not bothered much by the knowledge that any given goal is probably too difficult to achieve.

A flower pushing through the cracks of a sidewalk and stretching toward the sun doesn't worry overmuch about the fact that it'll only rise a few inches; it's just happy to be rising, and so am I.

For example, I had a few other ancillary goals in 2016; though discussing them is a bit of a distraction from our primary focus, I think a brief detour will help elucidate my point about motivation and goal magnitude. While working on the STEMpunk Project I tried to get a 500-pound deadlift, learn Russian, and read more primary sources in history. As of this writing I managed a 445-pound pull once last year, but knee and back problems have forced into the more modest 305- to 315-pound range; I *did* learn quite a bit of Russian, but not nearly as much as I'd hoped to; I explored a number of primary sources in political philosophy and history, but never quite got around to the ones I wanted to read.

So I failed, but at the same time those aren't bad numbers for deadlift, I now know a lot more Russian than I did in 2015, and I can start reading Carlyle's 'Latter Day Pamphlets' or Engels' 'The Condition of the Working Class in England' whenever I please.

In other words, I only managed to rise a few inches towards my better self, but rise I did.

Of course not everyone is going to feel the same way. Some people experience an acute sting when they fail to accomplish *exactly* what they set out to accomplish. If it isn't clear which of these categories you fall into you need to do some introspecting and find out, because that self-knowledge is extremely powerful. With it you can decide whether or not to just dive into a large project and hope for the best or to leave yourself enormous margins of error so as not to experience a net loss of motivation as you proceed.

In either case I would encourage you to at least *try* to keep your eyes on the bigger picture. Feelings of inadequacy can be very difficult to brush aside, but when they happen to me, there are a couple of things I keep in mind:

1) Everything I'm good at I used to not be good at.

I don't think it's unfair to say that at the peak of my guitar-playing abilities I was within sight of being world class. Around the age of 21 or 22 I could easily handle Andy Mckee's 'Drifting', and I had a pretty convincing cover of Eric Johnson's seminal 'Cliffs of Dover' under my belt. But even my original compositions were compelling and nuanced.

For this reason it eventually became easy to forget how bad I was when I started and how hard I had to work to achieve what I did. I think I had been 'playing' guitar for about two years before I even began to seriously practice. Even then, while my progress was fairly quick, it was far from spectacular.

The same man who went on to excel musically spent many, many frustrating hours trying to get graceless fingers to coax something vaguely resembling music out of an uncooperative piece of wood. Perhaps the same man who goes on to found a billion dollar company or helps reshape the foundations of AI theory will look back on simple coding exercises he once struggled with and wonder why it ever seemed so hard.

2) Constant failure is the price you pay for greatness.

A great way to avoid failure is to simply never try to do anything hard. You could just start working at a Barnes and Noble, wait until you're in middle management, and stay there for the next half century while experiencing very few embarrassing failures.

Since I've deliberately chosen not to take the easy way out, there's no avoiding the fact that I'm going to bump up against my limits. I'm going to embark on a project that'll wind up being too ambitious and at some point I'll simply crash and burn.

But so what? Point me to anyone who has achieved great things, like solving a longstanding problem or remaking an industry, that also managed to avoid failure while they did so.

The tricky part, of course, is remembering this when you're actually in the middle of an ongoing crisis.

3) Titans don't always feel like Titans

John Ferling's 'Almost a Miracle' is a fascinating history of the Revolutionary War which stuck in my mind because it imparted profound insight into the personality of George Washington.

Washington is about the closest thing American history has to a mythical figure. And yet he spent his entire life feeling insecure because of his lack of formal education -- his famous terseness is thought to derive from a concern that if he spoke too much the elites around him would realize how little he knew relative to them -- and he repeatedly questioned his suitably for the role he was asked to play in the war.

This is the man that went up against one of the greatest empires in the history of Earth and won, all while unsure as to whether he had the personal resources, wit, and wherewithal to succeed.

Why should any of us expect our own accomplishments to come easily?

I'll level with you: you're going to fail. That's what happens when you hold yourself to a high standard and reach for the best within you. That's what happens when you have the audacity to stretch towards the sun.

You have to know when to throw in the towel, of course; not every idea is worth pursuing. But in my experience the majority of people err on the side of quitting far too soon. Finding someone with *too* much persistence and grit is pretty rare.

There's another thing I remind myself of as a last resort. Because it's harsh I don't invoke it often, but it's nevertheless true, and sometimes *I* have to be the person who'll say the things that need saying.

After a while spent futilely groping toward a solution to a problem, when I want to just let go and sink into mediocrity, I'll think to myself:

If this is all it takes to break me, I would never have been worthy of greatness anyway.

Chapter 9
An Abstraction-Layer Multiverse

What follows is a series of loosely-connected essays on comput-ing, computer science, and computer hardware. These are not meant to be exhaustive or comprehensive, but instead simply represent a smattering of topics I explored while working on this module of the STEMpunk Project.

The essays are: 1) a discussion of the design for a computer I want to build; 2) an overview of computer 'anatomy', including e.g. CPUs and Storage; 3) a treatment of various ways humans can and will interact with computers.

As part of the Computing section of The STEMpunk Project I want-ed to design my next PC.

I still designed the system even though I didn't have the funds to build it as I believe this to be a useful exercise for the aspiring techie.

To get a feel for how this process works I did two things: first, I read a couple of books on DIY PC building, making note of the com-ponents the authors chose for various 'budget', 'mainstream', and 'extreme' systems, and then I tried to analyze the makeup of a few systems with which I am familiar.

These insights guided the choices I made for my own system[41].

---

[41] What follows is a breakdown of a hypothetical system I want to build. Everyone knows that computer components become out of date almost as soon as they are released, so the system I eventually *do* build will doubtless be very different from the one I'm describing.

Case:

There are a billion different options for PC cases, with stylistic variations beyond counting. You have steampunk cases, which range from fairly minimalist to exuberantly Baroque, gorgeous cases made out of wood, cases with insane paint jobs, and all manner of custom-built oddities in the shape of musical instruments, anime characters, spacecraft, and so on.

When I picture the ideal computer case I have this vision of a pure glass pyramid etched with runes or other arcane symbols. Maybe someday I'll be able to afford having it custom built, but for now I'll probably just use an NZXT H630, the same model that cages Eric Raymond's 'Great Beast' (though Raymond's was black and I prefer the glossy white version).

Internals:

I'd like to go ahead and build an 'extreme' system based on the $1500 gaming build described in the essay in this footnote[42]. The way I see it my needs are reasonably similar to the ones that motivated the author's choice in components, and while I plan on using my system more for design, editing, and visualization than gaming, I'd like to leave the option open.

The motherboard he chose is an ASUS Z170A, upon which is mounted a formidable Intel Core i5-6600K CPU and a CM Hyper 212 EVO cooler. The whole apparatus is powered by an EVGA SuperNOVA G2 750 Watt power supply.

'Kingston' was a name in RAM manufacturing that repeatedly came up, and this system will utilize their HyperX Fury 16 GB offering. I don't plan on using a RAID configuration for storage, and I like feeling like I have plenty of room to expand into, so I'll probably install a few terabytes worth of Seagate Barracuda XT2 hard drive.

---

[42] https://elitegamingcomputers.com/top-gaming-computers/#21

In the graphics card department the Gigabyte GTX 980 Ti should be able to handle anything I'm likely to throw at it, and the Crystal Sound 3 integrated audio card is more than enough for my purposes. I will probably spring for some decent 2.1 speakers from Logitech, like their Z623 model.

Using brand name mice, keyboards, and displays doesn't matter all that much to me. The ergonomic USB keyboard that I've been using for a year should suffice, but I have been thinking about giving optical trackballs a try as they reduce wrist strain and extraneous motion. I don't know the first thing about trackballs, but because I have seen Logitech products endorsed all over the place I might as well try out their Trackman Marble Trackball mouse.

While I don't have strong preferences for one monitor over another, I hate toggling between windows on a crowded screen, so I am willing to buy some extra screen real estate. This means that whatever n00b pwnage or data visualizations I might happen to be involved in will reach my eyeballs via two (or possibly three) 20 inch monitors.

Computer Anatomy[43]

CPUs

No matter what sort of computing device you're using the underlying component is the transistor, discussed in more detail in 'The Light Mandala' chapter. Each transistor can either have current flowing through it, corresponding to an 'on' state, or have no current flowing through it, corresponding to an 'off' state. Transistors can be assembled into *logic gates* which are able to do Boolean algebraic operations of arbitrary complexity. In modern computing systems billions of these little devices are packed onto a single silicon chip.

---

[43] You may have noticed that all of a sudden there is bold text that's also italicized. Italicized text marks new essays within a chapter, and as before bolded text marks new sections within an essay. Prior to section 2 all chapters were single essays, but the STEMpunk section has chapters which contain multiple essays, so I demarcated them with italic titles.

Many people call the central processing unit (CPU) the 'brain' of the computer, and that's true in a sense[44]. The CPU's constituent parts, the floating-point unit (FPU) and the arithmetic logical unit (ALU) handle floating-point and integer operations, respectively. They act on long strings of 1's and 0's to perform tasks such as adding numbers or displaying images on the screen.

Data enters the system through the data bus, which can be thought of as an enormous data highway with either thirty-two lanes or sixty-four lanes, depending on whether it sits within a 32-bit or 64-bit chip. The first stop in the CPU is the bus interface unit, responsible for taking data from the bus and sending it to the appropriate place in cache memory. Cache memory (simply called 'cache') are littles pieces of very small, very fast memory located within the CPU or nearby. This memory results in significant gains in CPU speed because the CPU doesn't have to go all the way to RAM whenever it requires a frequently-used piece of data.

If you're doing a mathematics research project you'd probably go and sit in the mathematics section at the university library, but you'd also take whatever books you continuously reference and put them within reach so you don't have to get up every time you need a piece of information. This stockpile of material would be analogous to a computer's RAM. If you have a book open *right next to your computer*, it would be analogous to cache. Like cache, accessing it takes virtually no time -- you merely have to glance over while you type; like cache, it's very small -- you only have space for one or two items before the area around you becomes distractingly cluttered[45].

As of this writing many systems have several cache layers. L1 cache is the located in the closest physical proximity to the CPU, with L2 and L3 caches being respectively farther away. Once data comes in from the bus, it's then inspected by a branch target buffer

---

[44] 'How Computers Work', Ron White, 10th edition.

[45] These analogized distances are not to scale. It would be more accurate to say that cache is a book sitting next to you, and the hard disk is on another planet.

which looks for places where the data can follow one of several different pathways.

Many -- possibly *most* -- programs have conditional statements which specify actions to take when various situations obtain. For example, a simple program might say 'for every integer between one and ten, if the integer is even, print it, otherwise skip it and move on'. The branch target buffer looks for places where such conditional statements exist and tries to predict on the basis of experience which paths the program will take.

Using this information the fetch/decode unit begins pulling in instructions in the specified order, where they are broken down into more easily managed pieces. These micro-operations are then lined up in the reorder buffer where a dispatch/execution unit checks to see if all the information required to execute the instruction is available. If it is, then the operations are executed and the results stored in the same location. If it isn't, then the processor begins searching for the data in nearby cache memory. As instructions are carried out the execution unit compares what is actually happening with what the branch target buffer *thought* would happen. In the case of a mistaken prediction new instructions are pulled into the reorder buffer and the branch target buffer is alerted to its mistake. In this way it learns to generate better predictions over time.

While all this is happening a retirement unit is also checking the operations in the reorder buffer. When a certain number have been successfully executed it sends the batch to RAM, where they begin their journey out into the wider computing system to move a game character's sword or calculate digits of pi.

One way to make computers faster is to make transistors smaller so that more of them fit into a given processor, and to add more processors to the system. There are ways of designing software, including low-level software like the operating system, to make use of the additional computing power. In the simplest possible terms, the OS and the software it's running must collude to split instructions and data into streams, each of which can be sent to different processors. But even if a given piece of software isn't coded to utilize multi-core processing the OS can simply allocate one processor to the program and use the leftover processes for some other operation. The result is still a net gain in speed and efficiency.

Motherboards

The motherboard (or mainboard) is essentially a large, printed sheet of layers of copper paths called traces[46]. Different layers are devoted to different tasks, such as carrying information between components, and by having these tasks split among distinct levels within the motherboard issues like electrical shorting at junctions can be avoided. This effort is to ensure that the CPU, RAM, graphics cards, audio cards, and so forth function as an integrated unit.

A motherboard resembles a scaled-down model of the industrial sector of a major city; components are either integrated directly into the board, as are capacitors, or plugged into various slots designed for them. Most boards ship with extra slots so that motivated users can upgrade their system's capacity down the road by simply purchasing the necessary card and putting it in the correct slot. In an act of creative inspiration to rival the best Edgar Allan Poe, this set of chips is collectively known as the *chipset*.

The chipset and its electron messengers generate a lot of heat as a waste product. To prevent the motherboard and the computer from bursting into flames seconds after booting up, the chassis houses a number of internal fans meant to redirect and dissipate warm air. A bare-bones systems likely won't require more than a few fans, but higher-end systems have higher-performance components and a concomitantly greater need for fans. There are even systems so aggressively powerful as to require liquid cooling -- evidently killing zombies and using machine-learning to predict stock market trends creates a lot of waste heat.

---

[46] https://mitseu.files.wordpress.com/2014/09/how-motherboards-work.pdf

Memory

A common point of confusion among computer novices is the distinction between *memory* and *storage*. *Memory* refers to RAM and storage refers to long-term hard drive storage. So when your computer geek friends discuss the 32 gigabytes of RAM in their systems they're talking about memory; when the throw around phrases like '1 terabyte hard drive', they're talking about storage.

As discussed a few paragraphs ago *random access memory* (RAM) can be thought of as the computer's analogue to short-term memory[47]. Data and code which are being actively used are stored in RAM so they needn't be continuously pulled from a storage disk, a process which would be slow both because it takes more time to access storage and because storage is much farther away from the CPU. The 'random' in 'random access memory' means that any arbitrary point within RAM can be accessed directly without reference to other points. Moreover, RAM is *volatile*, meaning that without a continuous source of power the data it contains is erased.

Though they do not fall under either the memory or storage label, *Read Only Memory* (ROM) and *Complementary Metal-Oxide Semiconductors* (CMOS) are worth mentioning here. In order to boot up successfully and maintain configurations over the long term a computer must have a way of storing code which is virtually never changed, even during long periods of stasis. RAM is volatile so it won't work, and while I don't know if it is *technically* feasible to use hard drive space for this purpose, I do know that accessing it would be agonizingly slow.

So it is to more intransigent technology that we turn. As its name implies ROM is meant to be written to once and almost never written to again. This makes it ideal for applications such as holding diagnostic code that can be used when a PC is badly malfunctioning,

---

[47] 'PC Hardware: A Beginner's Guide', Ron Gilster: https://abiiid.files.wordpress. com/2010/12/pc-hardware-a-beginners-guide.pdf

specifying startup procedures which kick in well before the operating system has woken up, and storing information which allows a CPU to work with a new piece of hardware. CMOS performs similar and sometimes overlapping duties, with the main difference being that it is easier to update a CMOS chip than it is to update other types of ROM.

Storage

If RAM is used to hold active programs and information, and ROM is used to hold startup code, storage is used for basically everything else. Your favorite movies, the novel you'll finish someday, pictures from a family reunion, and the carefully-assembled library of music which reflects your eclectic tastes all live as 1's and 0's on a hard drive somewhere. The way data are written to and accessed by storage is absolutely incredible; in fact, in the course of learning about the nuts and bolts of computer systems I was more awestruck at how powerful storage is than perhaps any other piece of hardware.

Magnetism is the secret to that power[48]. The actual 'storage' happens on a thin layer of metal which coats a disk-shaped *platter* made of aluminum or glass. Individual positions on this layer can either be magnetized or demagnetized, corresponding to a 1 or a 0, respectively. As the *read/write head* interacts with the platter it reads or writes these magnetized/demagnetized spots as binary code, not unlike magnetic braille. So when you pull up a movie from storage, the read/write head must find the series of 1's and 0's corresponding to the movie and read it off of the platter; likewise, when you download an mp3 to your hard drive the read/write head must find a stretch of empty space and write the 1's and 0's corresponding to the mp3 onto the platter.

If you spend a moment pondering how complicated movies are, then you'll appreciate how many 1's and 0's are required to capture one. For this reason organization is vitally important to the proper

---

[48]   http://www.explainthatstuff.com/harddrive.html

function of a hard drive. Data are not just written on any spare stretch of hard drive real estate but in *sectors*, which themselves are arranged into rings called *tracks*. Somewhere on the hard drive is a map specifying which sectors have been written to and which are still unused, allowing the hard drive to efficiently find space for writing new data.

Of course it's not possible to write enough data on a single platter to satisfy the average computer user's demand for storage. Platters therefore have read/write heads on both sides, and most hard drives contain stacks of platters arranged on a central column. A small gap is left between each platter to allow the read/write head to maneuver. In modern computing systems data usually aren't written *horizontally* across a single platter because accessing those data would require a lot of inefficient movement by the read/write head. Instead data are split vertically between platters in a *cylinder*. Some data will live on the first disk, some just below it on the second disk, some more just below that on the third disk, and so on. While this might be more difficult to conceptualize, it results in a net gain of hard drive speed because the read/write heads don't have to physically move through as much space.

I *told* you storage was amazing[49].

The Future of Human-Computer Interaction

If computers consisted only of mainboards, CPUs, storage, and memory, most people wouldn't give a damn about them. What places the remarkable abstraction-layer multiverse so squarely in the lives of millions of people is the fact that they're interactive. With a keyboard and a screen we can keep in touch with relatives backpacking in Asia, compose lengthy blog posts commenting on a recent election, reach out to our heroes through email, and waste hours refreshing our Facebook news feeds. In other words,

---

[49] Find more at: http://homepage.cs.uri.edu/faculty/wolfe/book/Readings/Reading05.htm,
http://computer.howstuffworks.com/computer-memory1.htm, http://www.explainingcomputers.com/storage.html

most people only really care about a computer's input/output (I/O) mechanisms.

While I had originally intended to include a section on mice, keyboards, scanners, printers, monitors, and all the other most common I/O devices, the truth is these are well documented elsewhere and are not as essential to a theoretical understanding of computer systems as the ones I did cover. Therefore, I decided to write instead about some novel I/O mechanisms which might be appearing on the horizon in the near future.

The QWERTY keyboard (so named for the first six letters on the top-left row) has been the undisputed emperor of computer interfaces since its invention by Christopher Latham Sholes in the latter part of the 19th century[50]. Though these days most computer users interact with their machines through a graphical user interface (GUI), power users, programmers, and serious computer enthusiasts choose the keyboard-based command-line interface (CLI). The CLI is a means for issuing commands to a computer with very short typed strings. 'mvdir' for example, is short for 'move directory'. This allows you move a file to another location with just a text command -- no mice, files, or folders involved.

While the CLI is slow and cumbersome at first, as you gain fluency it becomes not only more effective for common tasks, but also makes tractable many tasks that would be extremely tedious with just the GUI. A short CLI command lets you do things like find all the files above a certain size on the entire computer and copy them to a new location, for example.

It's unlikely, therefore, that the keyboard is going to disappear any time soon. But the following explores some alternatives to the standard QWERTY keyboard, beginning with different keyboard layouts and proceeding to ever-more-abstract territory.

---

[50] http://www.infoworld.com/article/2872529/computer-hardware/goodbye-keyboard-the-future-of-input-devices-is-almost-here.html#slide1 (this link also contains an abundance of information about other near-future I/O mechanisms)

By far the most widely-known non-QWERTY format is the Dvorak layout, named for its inventor August Dvorak[51]. As the story goes the original QWERTY scheme was devised to prevent early typewriters from jamming when adjacent keys were pressed in quick succession. By trying to maximize the distance between commonly-typed character sequences the QWERTY layout prevented this from happening as often, but for many people all that extra distance adds up to repetitive-stress injuries and discomfort. Dvorak built his layout so that the most commonly-used characters were on the 'home row', directly beneath the fingers, thus both theoretically reducing the amount of strain experienced by heavy typing sessions while also boosting typing speed. There hasn't been conclusive formal research into Dvorak, but anecdotal evidence and a few promising studies[52] support the assertion that it increases typing speed.

But key layouts are not the only possibilities explored by would-be reformers of keyboard design. While standard keyboards don't account for such factors as wrist positioning and finger length, keyboards which do have the potential to drastically reduce the chances of repetitive stress injuries. A company called Maltron specializes in building this kind of keyboard, and even has models which can be used one-handed (for typists only able to use one of their hands). The SafeType keyboard takes this concept even further, placing the majority of the keys in a vertical position so that it isn't even possible to put certain kinds of strain on your hands.

Of course ergonomics is not the only motivation for building alternative keyboards. The Optimus Maximus is a model whose every key contains a small LED screen indicating the function which is currently mapped to it. It's possible to simply have each key represent a letter or number, as in a standard keyboard, but it's also possible to map a nearly infinite variety of other commands to the keys, up to and including small programs or shortcuts in software like photoshop. The keys' LEDs even support GIFs. According to

---

[51] https://www.howtogeek.com/189270/alternative-keyboard-layouts-explained-dvorak-colemak-and-whether-you-should-care/

[52] http://atri.misericordia.edu/Papers/Dvorak.php

reviews typing on it takes a lot of force, so notwithstanding the fact that it could potentially spare a user a lot of typing it isn't built for a specifically ergonomic purpose[53] [54].

If the Optimus Maximus or QWERTY is too clunky it might soon be possible to leave physical input behind altogether. There are currently several ongoing attempts to engineer technology which would allow text-based interaction with computers in the complete absence of an actual keyboard. The AirType concept relies on sensors which wrap around both hands and which gradually learn a user's typing habits, making it possible to pen a scathing review directly on your desk or kitchen countertop[55]. Anyone who hasn't memorized key positions by heart might find it difficult to type with literally *nothing* to look at, so those folks must await the maturation of 'projection keyboard' technology, like the R2D2 virtual keyboard[56]. This lilliputian marvel of engineering uses a laser to generate an infrared keyboard which maps disturbances in its field to keystrokes, keeping pace with speeds of up to 350 words per minute -- the world's nerds will surely go into seizures upon reading that sentence.

It's safe to say that nearly everyone currently using a computer learned on a physical keyboard which you can actually *feel*, and it remains to be seen whether or not the lack of mechanical, haptic feedback will be an insuperable obstacle to widespread adoption of these technologies.

Of course we might view the Byzantine practice of using *keyboards*, virtual or otherwise, with disdain. The most plausible candidate for a keyboard-less input method is voice recognition,

---

[53] https://www.engadget.com/2008/02/22/optimus-maximus-at-long-last-we-bring-one-home-to-test/#/

[54] http://gizmodo.com/381011/ten-things-you-need-to-know-about-the-optimus-maximus-keyboard-hardware

[55] https://vimeo.com/90766615

[56] http://www.hammacher.com/Product/86110?PID=8200811&source=cj&utm_source=Affiliate&utm_medium=CPA&utm_campaign=C

a rather unreliable technology which in recent years has begun to stabilize. Doubtless you've seen commercials for voice recognition software which allows users to perform simple computer tasks like composing and sending emails. But there are now also people using voice recognition software to produce actual functioning code. The most famous example is Tavis Rudd, whose repetitive stress injuries drove him to use a python extension and standard voice recognition software to piece together a voice-based coding environment which is evidently so effective that he still uses it after his injuries have cleared up[57]. Since then there have been several other demonstrations of this technique and at least one attempt to create a language-agnostic general-purpose voice coding backend[58]. This is a space I've been watching with interest because of my own struggles with RSI.

Lying between or adjacent to the foregoing in the abstraction hierarchy is the exciting gesture recognition software now on the horizon. Noting astutely that hands are the original user interface, the Leap Motion team is endeavoring to build hand tracking software sophisticated enough to use in virtual reality (VR) and augmented reality (AR) applications[59].

An even more sophisticated version of this idea is 'the Ring', an aptly named device worn on the index finger and packed full of circuits and sensors which allow a user to perform innumerable tasks with just a few flicks of the wrist. Scribbling a phantom signature in the air has long been a signal to a waiter or waitress that you'd like your check. With the ring, this gesture actually initiates a payment app on your phone, drawing a dollar amount schedules a payment for that amount, and moving your finger to the right completes the transaction[60].

---

[57]   https://www.infoq.com/presentations/Programming-Voice#anch96728

[58]   https://voicecode.io/#about

[59]   https://www.leapmotion.com/about/#about-us

[60]   https://www.fastcodesign.com/3027206/a-ring-that-lets-you-control-pretty-much-anything-by-writing-in-the-air

But perhaps most exciting of all the technology in this class is 'SignAloud'[61], the invention of a pair of undergraduate students. These gloves were built to overcome the formidable barriers to communicating with the millions of deaf people in the world by translating American Sign Language into spoken words[62]. Previous attempts at this technology were either far too clunky or too unreliable for daily use, but the (relatively) slim, lightweight, and ergonomic gloves likely won't require too much engineering to be inconspicuous and comfortable.

Easily the most advanced technology in this tour of the near future is the suite of brain-computer interfaces being developed which hold the potential to allow direct control of computers with thought alone. NeuroSky makes headsets which use EEG readings to take pictures, play games, control helicopters, and cultivate zen-like focus[63]. The Defense Advanced Research Projects Agency (DARPA) is working on a prosthetic device which responds to neural commands, potentially opening the way for advanced medical solutions for amputees[64].

It seems clear that the logical conclusion of voice-, gesture-, and thought-recognition software is a magical user interface (MUI). What is 'wingardium leviosa' but a verbal command? What are tight, precise wand movements but gesture-based computing? And when your favorite song comes on the moment you want to hear it is there any practical difference between that and casting a spell? If we assume that magical systems are rule-based technologies with various methods of providing input then the drive to create smaller, less visible, more fluid ways of working with our devices could result in a future that resembles the worlds

---

[61] http://www.huffingtonpost.com/entry/navid-azodi-and-thomas-pryor-signaloud-gloves-translate-american-sign-language-into-speech-text_us_571fb38ae4b0f309baeee06d

[62] http://lemelson.mit.edu/sites/default/files/content/documents/awards/Student_Prize/LemelsonMIT_UseIt_Undergraduate_2016_FactSheet.pdf

[63] https://store.neurosky.com/

[64] http://www.darpa.mil/program/revolutionizing-prosthetics

we love to read about[65]. But this way, the underlying mechanisms will be comprehensible to anyone willing to do their own
STEMpunk Project.

---

[65]   Of course this presumes a modern, scientific understanding of 'magic'. In cultures with actual thaumaturgical traditions magic is/was understood differently,
and members of those cultures probably wouldn't agree with my claims.

Chapter 10
The Light Mandala

What follows is a series of loosely-connected essays on both electronics hardware and electronics theory. These are not meant to be exhaustive or comprehensive, but instead simply represent a smattering of topics I explored while working on this module of the STEMpunk Project.

The essays are: 1) my experiences with the Sparkfun Inventor's Kit; 2) an overview of basic electronics theory; 3) a catalogue of the most fundamental electronics components; 4) batteries; 5) transistors; 6) the differences between inductors, capacitors, and batteries; 7) and a brief essay about a time I tried to diagnose a hardware failure which illustrates how this project has changed my thinking.

The Sparkfun Inventor's Kit

The electronics module of The STEMpunk Project began when I excitedly tore open my Sparkfun Inventor's Kit (SIK) and plugged the Redboard into my computer. Once I overcame some initial difficulties and got the SIK working I knocked out all sixteen project circuits in about three days and took some pictures as I went along. In each picture the 'breadboard' is the white rectangle connected to the red circuit board and located to the left of my computer.

This is circuit one, just a simple little LED light:

Circuit two contains a potentiometer -- basically a knob for adjusting voltage -- which gave me the power to brighten or dim the LED. See it there on the breadboard?

Circuit eight powered a small servo motor with a propeller attached. It's sitting to the right of the breadboard:

Circuit fifteen displayed a 'hello world' message on the tiny LCD screen. It's pretty tough to see the screen, but it's plugged into the breadboard on the right side and hanging over the edge a little bit:

The final circuit, number sixteen, coded a simple memory game where I had to use the buttons to replay a pattern produced by the LED lights:

Foundations in Electronics Theory

CABLES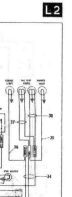

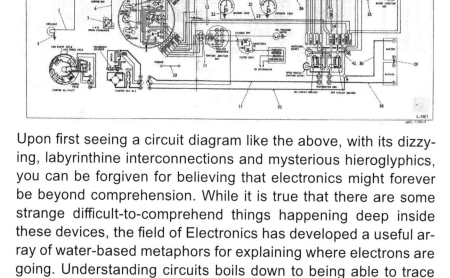

Upon first seeing a circuit diagram like the above, with its dizzying, labyrinthine interconnections and mysterious hieroglyphics, you can be forgiven for believing that electronics might forever be beyond comprehension. While it is true that there are some strange difficult-to-comprehend things happening deep inside these devices, the field of Electronics has developed a useful array of water-based metaphors for explaining where electrons are going. Understanding circuits boils down to being able to trace the interactions of four basic forces: voltage, current, resistance, and power.

Voltage, measured in volts, is often analogized as being like water pressure in a hose. For a given hose with a set diameter and length, more water pressure is going to mean more water flow and less water pressure is going to mean less water flow. If two 100-gallon tanks, one empty and one full, are connected by a length of pipe with a shutoff valve at its center, the water in the full tank is going to exert a lot of pressure on the valve because it 'wants' to flow into the empty tank.

Voltage is essentially electrical pressure, or, more technically, a difference in electrical potential. The negative terminal of a battery contains many electrons which, because of their like charges, are repelling each other and causing a buildup of pressure. Like the water in the 100-gallon tank they 'want' to flow through the conductor to the positive terminal.

Current, measured in amps, is the amount of electricity flowing past a certain point in one second, not unlike the amount of water flowing through a hose. If more pressure (i.e. 'voltage') is applied, then current goes up, and correspondingly drops if pressure decreases. Returning to our two water tanks, how could we increase water pressure so as to get more water to flow? By replacing the full 100-gallon tank with a full 1000-gallon tank!

But neither the water in the pipe nor the current in the wire flows unimpeded. Both encounter *resistance*, measured in ohms when in a circuit, in the form of friction from their respective conduits. No matter how many gallons of water we put in the first tank, the pipe connecting them only has so much space through which water can move, and if we increase the pressure too much the pipe will simply burst. But if we increase its diameter, its resistance decreases and more water can flow through it *at the same amount of pressure*.

At this point you may be beginning to sense the basic relationship between voltage, current, and resistance. If we increase voltage we get more current because voltage is like pressure, but this can only be pushed so far because the conductor exhibits resistance to the flow of electricity. Getting a bigger wire means we can get more current at the same voltage, or more means we can increase current to get even more current.

If only there were some simple, concise mathematical representation of all this! There is, and it's called Ohm's Law: $V = IR$. Here 'V' means voltage, 'I' means current, and 'R' means resistance. This equation says that voltage is directly proportional to the product of current and resistance. Some basic algebraic manipulations yield other useful equations: $I = V/R$, or $R = V/I$, for example.

From these we can see clearly what before we were only grasping with visual metaphors. Current is directly proportional to voltage: more pressure means more current. It is indirectly proportional to resistance: more resistance means less current. Knowing any two of these values allows us to solve for the other.

That last fundamental force we need to understand is power. In physics, *power* is defined as 'the ability to do work'. Pushing a rock up a hill requires a certain amount of power, and pushing a bigger rock up a hill, or the same rock up a steeper hill, requires more power.

For our purposes power, measured in watts, can be represented by this equation: $P = VI$. You have a given amount of electrical pressure (V) and a given amount of electrical flow (I), and together they give you the ability to turn a lightbulb on. As before we can rearrange the terms in this equation to generate other useful insights: $I = P/V$, or $V = P/I$.

From this we can deduce, for example, that for a 1000 watt appliance increasing the voltage allows us to draw less current. This is very important if you're trying to do something like build a flower nursery and need to know how many lights will be required, how many watts will be used by each light, and how many amps and volts can be supplied to your building.

There you have it! No matter how complicated a power grid or the avionics on a space shuttle might seem, everything boils down to how power, voltage, current, and resistance interact.

Basic Electrical Components

Circuits can be things of stupefying power and complexity, responsible for everything from changing channels on t.v. to controlling spacecraft as they exit the outer boundaries of the solar system.

But for all that, there are a handful of basic components found in very nearly every circuit on the planet. An understanding of these components can go a long way toward making electronics more comprehensible.

Resistors

Resistors have the charming quality of doing exactly what their name implies, i.e. they *resist* the flow of electrons in a circuit. This is useful for keeping LEDs within acceptable ranges so they light up but don't blow out, for creating voltage dividers for use in resistive components like photocells or flex sensors, and for incorporating things like buttons into circuits through the use of pull-up resistors.

More:

1. Sparkfun's resistor tutorial[66] is carefully done and is the source of the examples of resistors cited in the above paragraph.

2. Resistorguide's thorough exploration[67] of resistors is notable for its discussion of different kinds of resistors and the pros and cons of using each.

3. ScienceOnline's tutorial[68] carefully walks through how to interpret the colored bands found on most resistors, and demonstrates the effect on an LED's brightness of running the same current through different resistors. It also notes that graphite is similar to the material used to make resistors, and does two fascinating little experiments with pencil marks on paper acting as a resistor in a circuit.

4. GreatScott's resistor video[69] repeats much of the information in the other videos but succinctly explains what pull-up and pull-down resistors are.

---

[66] https://learn.sparkfun.com/tutorials/resistors

[67] https://www.youtube.com/watch?v=Gc1wVdbVl0E

[68] https://www.youtube.com/watch?v=HrZZMhWZiFk

[69] https://www.youtube.com/watch?v=7w5l-KbJ1Sg

Capacitors

Capacitors come in a wide variety of styles -- ceramic disk, polyfilm, electrolytic -- but all are designed to exploit properties of electro-magnetic fields to store electrical charge. They are built by separating two conductive plates either with space or with a nonconducting material called a dielectric. When current is applied to a circuit with a capacitor, negative charge piles up on one plate. The dielectric won't conduct electricity but it can support an electric field, which gets stronger as electrons accrue on one side of the capacitor. This causes positive charges to gather on the other plate, and the electric field between the positively- and negatively-charged plates stores a proportional amount of power, which can later be discharged.

More:

1. Collin Cunningham elucidates[70] capacitors by ripping one apart, delving briefly into their history, and then constructing one from a pill bottle and some aluminum foil.

2. HumanHardDrive approaches[71] capacitors and capacitance from a theoretical standpoint, delving into the chemistry and math involved.

3. Eugene Khutoryansky offers an even more granular look[72] at what's going on inside capacitors.

Inductors

Like capacitors, inductors store electrical energy. A typical inductor will be made up of metal wire wrapped around something like an iron bar. When current is applied to an inductor a magnetic field begins to build and when current is cut off it begins to disintegrate. As a rule magnetic fields don't like changing, so the generated field

---

[70]   https://www.youtube.com/watch?v=ZYH9dGl4gUE

[71]   https://www.youtube.com/watch?v=spuf53W8ckE

[72]   https://www.youtube.com/watch?v=f_MZNsEqyQw

resists the initial increase in current and the later decrease in current. Once current levels off, however, the inductor will act like a normal wire for as long as the current doesn't change. Induction motors exploit these electromagnetic properties to generate torque for applications like spinning fan blades.

More:

1. Eugene Khutoryansky does another fantastic job in his video[73] on the behavior of inductors in a circuit.

2. Afrotechmods spends a lot of time demonstrating[74] how current changes in response to different inductance values.

Diodes

Diodes are small semiconductors whose purpose in life is to allow current to flow in one direction only. If a negative voltage is applied to a diode it is *reverse-biased* ('off') and no current can flow, but if zero or positive voltage is applied it is *forward-biased* ('on') and current can flow from its anode terminal to its cathode terminal. If enough negative voltage is applied to the diode, it is possible for current to begin flowing *backwards*, from the cathode terminal to the anode terminal.

More:

1. Sparkfun's very thorough introduction[75] to diodes.

2. Collin Cunningham of MAKE magazine returns to explain[76] the basics of diode function.

---

[73] https://www.youtube.com/watch?v=ukBFPrXiKWA

[74] https://www.youtube.com/watch?v=NgwXkUt3XxQ

[75] https://learn.sparkfun.com/tutorials/diodes

[76] https://www.youtube.com/watch?v=AqzYsuTRVRc

Batteries

When I wrote the previous section I wanted to include batteries and transistors as well. As research progressed however it occurred to me that these latter two devices were very complex and would require their own discussion. Here I want to cover a remarkable little invention familiar to everyone: batteries.

Battery Basics

The two fundamental components of a battery are electrodes and an electrolyte, which together make up one cell. The electrodes are made of different metals whose respective properties give rise to a difference in electrical potential energy which can be used to induce current flow. These electrodes are then immersed in an electrolyte, which can be made from a sulfuric acid chemical bath, a gel-like paste, or many other materials. When an external conductor is hooked up to each electrode current will flow from one of them (the 'negative terminal') to the other (the 'positive terminal').

Battery cells can be primary or secondary, and are distinguished by whether or not the chemical reactions happening in the cell cause one of the terminals to erode. The simplest primary cell consists of a zinc electrode as the negative terminal, a carbon electrode as the positive terminal, and sulfuric acid diluted with water as the electrolyte. As current flows zinc molecules combine with sulfuric acid to produce zinc sulfate and hydrogen gas, thus consuming the zinc electrode.

But even when not connected to a circuit impurities in the zinc electrode can cause small amounts of current to flow in the electrode and correspondingly slow rates of erosion to occur. This is called local action and is the reason why batteries can die even when not used for long periods of time. Of course there exist techniques for combating this, like coating the zinc electrode in mercury to pull out impurities and render them less reactive. None of these work flawlessly, but advances in battery manufacturing have allowed for the creation of long-storage batteries with a sealed electrolyte, released only when the battery is actually used, and of primary cell batteries that can be recharged.

A secondary cell works along the same chemical principles as a primary cell, but the electrodes and electrolyte are composed of materials that don't dissolve when they react. In order to be classifiable as 'rechargeable' it must be possible to safely reverse the chemical reactions inside the cell by means of running a current through it in the reverse direction of how current normally flows out of it. Unlike the zinc-carbon voltaic cell discussed above, for example, in a nickel-cadmium battery the molecules formed during battery discharge are easily reverted to their original state during recharging[77].

Naturally it is difficult to design and build such a sophisticated electrochemical mechanism, which is why rechargeable batteries are more expensive.

Combining Batteries in Series or in Parallel

Like most other electrical components batteries can be hooked up in series, in parallel, or in series-parallel. To illustrate, imagine four batteries lined up in a row, with their positive terminals on the left and their negative terminals on the right. If wired in series, the negative terminal on the rightmost battery would be the negative terminal for the whole apparatus and the positive terminal on the leftmost battery would be the positive terminal for the whole apparatus. In between, the positive terminals of one battery are connected to the negative terminals of the next battery, causing the voltage of the individual batteries to be cumulative. This four-battery setup would generate six volts total (1.5V per battery multiplied by the number of batteries), and the total current of the circuit load (a light bulb, a radio, etc.) is non-cumulative and would flow through each battery.

---

[77] Much more information on the underlying chemistry at: https://www.scientificamerican.com/article/how-do-rechargeable-that/

If wired in parallel, the positive and negative terminals of the right-most battery would connect to the same terminal on the next battery, and the terminals for the leftmost battery would connect to the external circuit. In this setup it is voltage which is non-cumulative and current which is cumulative. By manipulating and combining these properties of batteries it is possible to supply power to a wide variety of circuit configurations.

Different Battery Types

Nickel Cadmium: NiCd batteries are a mature technology and thus well-understood. They have a long life but relatively low energy density and are thus suited for applications like biomedical equipment, radios, and power tools. They do contain toxic materials and aren't eco-friendly.

Nickel-Metal Hydride: NiMH batteries have a shorter life span and correspondingly higher energy density. Unlike their NiCd cousins NiMH batteries contain nothing toxic.

Lead Acid: Lead Acid batteries tend to be very heavy and so are most suitable for use in places where weight isn't a factor, like hospital equipment, emergency lighting, and automobiles.

Absorbent Glass Mat: The AGM is a special kind of lead acid battery in which the sulfuric acid electrolyte is absorbed into a fine fiberglass mesh. This makes the battery spill proof and capable of being stored for very long periods of time. They are also vibration resistance and have a high power density, all of which combine to make them ideal for high-end motorcycles, NASCAR, military vehicles, RVs, golf carts, off-grid storage, and a variety of other applications.

Lithium Ion: Li-on is the fastest growing battery technology. Being high-energy and very lightweight makes them ideal for laptops and smartphones.

Lithium Ion Polymer: Li-on polymer batteries are very similar to plain Li-on batteries but ever smaller.

The Future of Batteries

Batteries have come a very long way since Ewald Von Kleist first stored static charge in a Leyden jar in 1744. Lithium Ion seems to be the hot topic of discussion, but there are efforts being made at building aluminum batteries, solid state batteries, and microbatteries, and some experts maintain that the exciting thing to watch out for is advances in battery manufacturing.

Hopefully before long we'll have batteries which power smart clothing and extend the range of electric vehicles to thousands of miles.

Transistors

The development of the transistor began out of a need[78] to find a superior means of amplifying telephone signals sent through long-distance wires. Around the turn of the twentieth century American Telephone and Telegraph (AT&T) had begun offering transcontinental telephone service as a way of staying competitive. The signal boost required to allow people to talk to each other over thousands of miles was achieved with triode vacuum tubes based on the design of Lee De Forest, an American inventor. But these vacuum tubes consumed a lot of power, produced a lot of heat, and were unreliable to boot. Mervin Kelly of Bell Labs recognized the need for an alternative and, after WWII, began assembling the team that would eventually succeed.

Credit for pioneering the transistor[79] is typically given to William Shockley, John Bardeen, and Walter Brattain, also of of Bell Labs, but they were not the first people to file patents for the basic transistor principle: Julius Lilienfeld filed one for the field-effect transistor in 1925 and Oskar Hiel filed one in 1934. Neither man made much of an impact in the growing fields of electronics theory or electronics manufacturing, but there is evidence that William Shockley and

---

[78]   http://www.pbs.org/transistor/album1/

[79]   https://en.wikipedia.org/wiki/History_of_the_transistor

Gerald Pearson, a co-worker at Bell Labs, did build a functioning transistor prototype from Lilienfeld's patents.

Shockley, Brattain, and Bardeen understood that if they could solve certain basic problems they could build a device that would act like a signal amplifier in electronic circuits by exploiting the properties of semiconductors to influence electron flow.

Actually accomplishing this, of course, proved fairly challenging. After many failed attempts and cataloging much anomalous behavior a practical breakthrough was achieved[80]. A strip of the best conductor, gold, was attached to a plastic wedge and then sliced with a razor, producing two gold foil leads separated by an extremely small space. This apparatus was then placed in contact with a germanium crystal which had an additional lead attached at its base. The space separating the two pieces of gold foil was just large enough to prevent electron flow. Unless, that is, current were applied to one of the gold-tipped leads, which caused 'holes' -- i.e. spaces without electrons -- to gather on the surface of the crystal. This allowed electron flow to begin between the base lead and the other gold-tipped lead. The resulting device became known as the point-contact transistor, and gained the trio a Nobel Prize.

Though the point-contact transistor showed promise and was integrated with a number of electrical devices it was still fragile and impractical at a larger scale. This began to change when William Shockley developed an entirely new kind of transistor based on a 'sandwich' design. The result was essentially a precursor to the bipolar junction transistor, which is what almost everyone in the modern era means by the term 'transistor'.

Under the Hood

In the simplest possible terms a transistor is essentially a valve for controlling the flow of electrons. Valves can be thought of as

---

[80] https://en.wikipedia.org/wiki/Point-contact_transistor

amplifiers[81]: when you turn a faucet handle, force produced by your hand is amplified to control the flow of thousands of gallons of water, and when you press down on the accelerator in your car, the pressure of your foot is amplified to control the motion of thousands of pounds of fire and steel.

Valves, in other words, allow small forces to control much bigger forces. Transistors work in a similar way.

One common type of modern transistor is the bipolar junction NPN transistor, a cladistic descendant of Shockley's original design. It is constructed from alternating layers of silicon which are doped with impurities to give them useful characteristics.

In its pure form silicon is a textbook semiconductor. It contains four electrons in its valence shell which causes it to form very tight crystal lattices that typically don't facilitate the flow of electrons. The N layer is formed by injecting trace amounts of phosphorus, which contains five valence electrons, into this lattice. It requires much less energy to knock this fifth electron loose than it would to knock loose one of the four valence electrons in the silicon crystal, making the N layer semiconductive. Similarly, the P layer is formed by adding boron which, because of the three electrons in its valence shell, leaves holes throughout the silicon into which electrons can flow.

It's important to bear in mind that neither the P nor the N layers are electrically charged. Both are neutral and both permit greater flow of electrons than pure silicon would. The interface between the N and P layers quickly becomes saturated as electrons from the phosphorus move into the holes in the valence shell of the Boron. As this happens it becomes increasingly difficult for electrons to flow between the N and P layers, and eventually a boundary is formed. This is called the 'depletion layer'

Now, imagine that there is a 'collector' lead attached to the first N layer and another 'emitter' lead attached to the other N layer. Current cannot flow between these two leads because the depletion layer at

---

[81]   https://www.youtube.com/watch?v=W8hqr5X5ii0

the P-N junction won't permit it. Between these two layers, however, there is a third lead, called a 'base', placed very near the P layer. By making the base positively charged electrons can overcome the P-N junction and begin flowing from the emitter to the collector.

The key here is to realize that the amount of charge to the base required to get current moving is much smaller than the current flowing to the collector, and that current flow can be increased or decreased by a corresponding change in the current to the base. This is what gives the transistor its amplifier properties.

Transistors and Moore's Law

Even more useful than this, however, is the ability of a transistor to act as a switch[82]. Nothing about the underlying physics changes here. If current is not flowing in the transistor it is said to be in 'cut-off', and if current is flowing in the transistor it is said to be in 'saturation'. This binary property of transistors makes them ideally suited for the construction of logic gates, which are the basic components of every computer ever made.

A full discussion of logic gate construction would be well outside the purview of this essay, but it is worth briefly discussing one popular concept which requires a knowledge of transistors in order to be understood.

Named after Intel co-founder Gordon Moore, Moore's Law is sometimes stated as the rule that computing power will double roughly every two years[83]. The more accurate version is that the number of transistors which can fit in a given unit area will double every two years. These two definitions are fairly similar, but keeping the latter in mind will allow you to better understand the underlying technology and where it might head in the future.

---

[82] https://www.allaboutcircuits.com/textbook/semiconductors/chpt-4/transistor-switch-bjt/

[83] http://www.extremetech.com/extreme/210872-extremetech-explains-what-is-moores-law

Moore's law has held for as long as it has because manufacturers have been able to make transistors smaller and smaller. Obviously this can't continue forever, both because at a certain transistor density power consumption and heat dissipation become serious problems, and because at a certain size effects like quantum tunneling prevent the sequestering of electrons.

A number of alternatives to silicon-based chips are being seriously considered as a way of extending Moore's Law. Because of how extremely thin it can be made, graphene is one such contender. The problem, however, is that the electrophysical properties of graphene are such that building a graphene transistor that can switch on and off is not straightforward. A graphene-based computer, therefore, might well have to develop an entirely different logical architecture to perform the same tasks as modern computers.

Other potentially fruitful avenues are quantum computing, optical computing, and DNA computing, all of which rely on very different architectures than conventional Von-Neumann computers.

More:

1. Veritasium does a lively and entertaining explanation of transistor fundamentals.[84]

2. Despite his ominous name I found Ben Eater's transistor video informative.[85]

3. The lovable and eccentric Collin Cunningham strikes again![86]

Bottled Lightning

When I first began learning about basic electrical components I had a hard time distinguishing between inductors, capacitors, and batteries because they all appear to do the same thing: store

---

[84] https://www.youtube.com/watch?v=IcrBqCFLHIY

[85] https://www.youtube.com/watch?v=DXvAlwMAxiA

[86] https://www.youtube.com/watch?v=-td7YT-Pums

energy. As the inner workings of these devices became less opaque, however, myriad differences came into view. To help the beginner avoid some of my initial confusion here is a brief treatment of all three.

Though inductors, capacitors, and batteries do indeed store energy their means of doing so vary tremendously. This has implications for how quickly they can be charged, how quickly they can discharge, when and where they are most appropriately used, what future developments we can expect, etc.

Inductors store energy *electromagnetically*.[87] Though there is some controversy over the specific mechanics of energy storage in an inductor, most seem to agree that it relies on the magnetic field that is created when current runs through the inductor wire. As current increases the magnetic field increases, opposing the change in the current and absorbing energy in the process. When current levels off the magnetic field just sits there, holding on to its energy stores and not hassling the electrons as they flow through. But when current begins *decreasing* the magnetic field begins to collapse, and its energy goes towards keeping the electrons flowing. Thus the energy stored in the initial buildup of current is discharged when current begins to slow down.

Capacitors store energy *electrostatically*.[88] A basic capacitor is two conductive plates separated by an insulator, like air or micah. When current begins to flow onto one of these plates there is a build up of electrons and a resulting negative charge. On the other plate, electrons are drawn away both by the repulsive force of the electrons on the first plate and the attractive force of the positive terminal of the voltage source. As this is happening the orbits of the electrons of the atoms in the insulator separating the two plates begin to warp, spending more time near the positively-charged plate. Energy is

---

[87] https://electronics.stackexchange.com/questions/161457/how-does-an-inductor-store-energy

[88] https://electronics.stackexchange.com/questions/75151/does-a-capacitor-store-charge

thus stored in the field between the plates in a way similar to how energy is stored in a compressed spring.

Batteries store energy electrochemically.[89] As I've written before the simplest kind of battery consists of two electrodes made of different materials immersed in an electrolyte bath. The electrodes must be made such that one is more likely to give up electrons than the other. When a load is attached to the battery electrons flow from the 'negative' terminal through the load to the 'conductor'. Unlike inductors and capacitors batteries bring all their charge to the circuit in the beginning.

Literally Reducing a (Black) Box

I have described The STEMpunk Project as 'an exercise in black box reduction', by which I mean the project's bread and butter is making sense of the previously mysterious inner workings of the objects which make up daily life.

Once I took this phrase more literally by ripping apart a malfunctioning box fan. As it had sputtered to a stop in the heat of a June day I thought I might try my hand at fixing it, or at least divining how it worked. After pulling the coverings off the motor I took one look at its components and, not seeing any belts or pulleys, immediately thought 'magnets are involved somehow'.

Some quick googling confirmed my suspicions. The blades in many types of fans are spun via *induction motors*, remarkably clever devices which utilize rotating magnetic fields to generate torque. There are different types of induction motors, but one common variant is comprised of three pairs of coiled copper wire which generate a magnetic field when current is applied to them. Applying current to the next pair generates a new magnetic field with a new north pole a few degrees away from the previous north pole. The same process is repeated over and over again in each of the three pairs,

---

[89] http://www.scientificamerican.com/article/how-do-batteries-store-an/

causing a disk or cylinder positioned at the center of the apparatus to spin along with the magnetic field.

I have found this process of gradually discovering the intricacy of things I'd previously taken for granted to be enormously gratifying.

More:

1. Learning Engineering's 'Electrical Machines' playlist.[90]

---

[90] https://www.youtube.com/playlist?list=PLuUdFsbOK_8qVROrfl2M2WSV2x Az-ABVU

Chapter 11
A Dance of Fire and Steel

What follows is a series of loosely-connected essays on mechanics. These are not meant to be exhaustive or comprehensive, but instead simply represent a smattering of topics I explored while working on this module of the STEMpunk Project.

The essays are: 1) a discussion of my experiences building models; 2) an overview of internal combustion engines; 3) alternative combustion engine designs; 4) electric cars; 5) rocket engines.

The mechanics module involved more actual construction than any other, with the possible exception of the electronics module. As you can imagine, this was both fun and informative.

Before I even began the STEMpunk Project I bought and assembled a Smithsonian model car engine to try and calibrate how long it would take me to finish such a task[91]. Later, I assembled cars, cranes, and other models from an erector set. Here are some pictures of just a few of these creations:

---

[91] Alas, the pictures I took of that project aren't around anymore.

'How Cars Work' by Nick Arnold was a neat little children's book which included some models of simple car systems with brightly-colored pieces were large enough for children to handle. Here are brakes, suspension, and steering column:

  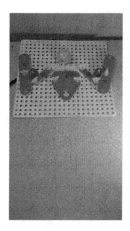

And I also built a scale model of a jet engine:

I would encourage you to play with kids toys if you're deciding to learn a STEM subject. Just because they're designed for children *doesn't* mean they aren't sophisticated and doesn't mean that they won't be beyond your skill level. How confident are you that you know all the chemistry from a chemistry set off the top of your head, right now? If your answer is 'no' then you'd benefit from owning and using one. And because they're designed with kids in mind they're often safe and feature very basic explanations of the relevant phenomena.

The idea of building models like this struck me as a little silly at first. But many a great engineer or physicist has gotten her start in exactly this way. There's no shame in following suit.

The Internal Combustion Engine

After beginning the Mechanics module I naturally began thinking about internal combustion engines, intriguing devices that can be found in a variety of machines ranging from lawnmowers to speed boats. All of them rely on the exothermic chemical process known as *combustion*, which occurs *internally*, hence their name.

The majority of vehicles on the road are propelled by a four-stroke spark-ignition internal combustion engine. Vehicles on the less powerful end of the scale might only sport 3- or 4-cylinder engines while those at the other extreme contain 8- or even 16-cylinder engines.

There are a few different ways to arrange these cylinders within the engine block. In an inline configuration the cylinders are in a row, as the name suggests. Obviously there is a limit to how many cylinders can be made to fit in a straight line under the hood, so many engines have their cylinders in a 'V' shape (hence the term 'V8'). One arm of the V will contain half the cylinders and the other arm will contain the other half, making better use of the space available. Less common than this are engines which have their cylinders lying sideways and the pistons moving left-to-right instead of up-and-down.

Each cylinder houses a *piston*, which is a metal drum that compresses the fuel-air mixture as it enters the cylinder cavity (also called the *cylinder bore*) and pushes exhaust out at the end of a full cycle. Each piston is connected to the *crankshaft* via a *connecting rod*, and it is the crankshaft which keeps all the pistons moving in sync. To prevent oil from leaking into the cylinder bore and exhaust from leaking out, each piston is wrapped in a set of rings which seals it in.

Internal combustion engines do not run on gasoline alone, but rather a mixture of air and gasoline together. In older vehicles and in simple, modern machines, the mixing of air and fuel is accomplished with a *carburetor*, but these days a *fuel-injection system* is more common. Air is brought into the engine and distributed to each cylinder by a series of tubes called an *intake (or inlet) manifold*. These come in numerous shapes, but a simple way to visualize the archetypal manifold for a V8 engine is as a cylindrical octopus laying on top of the engine with one leg going to every cylinder.

Four-stroke engines are so called because each piston turns fuel into motion by going through four distinct strokes: intake, compression, power, and exhaust. During *intake* an *intake valve* at the top of the cylinder bore opens and the fuel-air mixture is drawn into the cylinder cavity by the downward motion of the piston. The piston then moves upward during *compression*, crushing the mixture into 1/8th or 1/10th its original volume, depending on the engine's *compression ratio*. Then a *spark plug* ignites the mixture, beginning the 'power' phase. The subsequent explosion drives the piston downward, with the resulting force being distributed to the tires and causing them to rotate.

Now the cylinder bore is filled with carbon dioxide, water vapor, and other combustion byproducts, and an *exhaust valve* opens at the top of the cylinder bore to allow the upward motion of the piston to expel them.

The spectacular synchronization between intake valves, exhaust valves, and pistons is achieved in part by a *camshaft*. The camshaft is a metal rod with tear-drop shaped *lobes* attached to it, each one of which connects through a *rocker arm* to either an intake valve or an exhaust valve. Rocker arms have a long side and a short side, and as the camshaft spins one lobe presses against the short side of a rocker arm which causes the long side to descend and open a valve.

These valves are spring loaded, so when the camshaft rotates and the lobe disengages its rocker arm the valve shuts again. Taken together the camshaft, valves, and rocker arms are called the *valvetrain*, and are connected to the crankshaft by a *timing belt* which keeps their motion in tune.

The result can be viewed as an exquisitely timed dance of fire and steel: a piston expels exhaust through an exhaust valve opened by a rocker arm, and is thus ready to begin its cycle anew; the crankshaft rotates, and the piston is drawn downward by its connecting rod; the camshaft rotates, synchronized to the crankshaft by a timing belt, and one of its lobes touches a rocker arm which opens the intake valve for the piston; the fuel-air mixture enters the cylinder bore, sucked in by the piston's descent; the crankshaft continues to spin, now pushing the piston upward and compressing the mixture into a tiny space; there comes a spark, and an explosion, which fires the piston downward with great violence; the vehicle moves; the camshaft, bound by the timing belt to the crankshaft, now uses a different rocker arm to open the exhaust valve; the crankshaft sends the piston skyward again, and the exhaust is expelled.

This process naturally generates enormous amounts of friction. The engine is able to withstand this because much of its surface area is coated with *oil*, which in addition to lubrication also serves to marginally cool the engine down. The engine's oil reservoir is called a *sump*, and usually sits below the crankshaft. An *oil pump* sends the oil to an *oil filter* before it is distributed by *oil channels* to the crankshaft bearings, cylinder bore, valvetrain, and anywhere else metal is touching metal. After performing its job the oil returns to the sump to be sent through the cycle again. Like everything oil breaks down eventually, which is why it must be regularly changed to keep the engine running smoothly.

But the cooling effects of oil are very minor compared to the tremendous amounts of heat created by combustion, which means that engines require an additional dedicated *cooling system*. While it is possible to air cool an engine, most vehicles rely on liquid cooling.

As the coolant of choice, water sits in a plastic tank waiting to be pumped throughout the engine. Because vehicles are expected to operate year round in a variety of different conditions the coolant must be protected from extreme cold by antifreeze and from extreme heat by being pressurized enough to push its boiling point up into a safe range.

A *water pump* sends the coolant through a number of hoses which spread like blood vessels through the engine, absorbing heat. When the coolant has absorbed as much heat as it is designed to, it is sent to the *radiator*. Consisting of many thin, usually horizontal tubes, the radiator is designed to 'spread' the coolant out so that it releases the heat it has absorbed into the air, effectively carrying it away from the engine. Proper heat dissipation requires there to be a constant stream of air running over the radiator's tubing; this is simple when the vehicle is going fast, but small electric fans are required to maintain airflow when the vehicle is going slow or at a stop.

Modern engines make use of ingenious devices to maintain the appropriate coolant pressure and temperature. The *radiator pressure cap* is built so that when pressure exceeds a certain threshold a small amount of coolant is let out into a reserve tank where it waits until it can be reintroduced into the cooling system. The mechanical *thermostat* is calibrated to open only when the coolant reaches a certain temperature. If the coolant is still cool it is recirculated through the engine, but if it has gotten hot it is sent to the radiator to cool down.

How then does the engine receive the initial spark it requires to turn over? Usually a lead-acid battery and an induction coil are used together to begin ignition, after which point the engine is somewhat self-sustaining. As the engine runs it spins an *alternator*, which is just a small generator inside the car that feeds energy back to the battery.

Alternative Internal Combustion Engine Designs

As it turns out there are a number of variations on the standard internal combustion engine (ICE) design, and to satisfy my curiosity I researched several less common such adaptations. To avoid excessive wordiness I will refer to the most common gasoline-powered internal combustion engine as an ICE, even though technically every engine below is an ICE.

Diesel Engine

Diesel engines and ICEs are pretty similar. The biggest difference is that, while an ICE draws the fuel-air mixture into a cylinder bore all at once, this process occurs in two stages in a diesel engine. Air is drawn into the cylinder bore during intake and fuel is injected near the end of compression. Diesel engines have no spark plugs; instead, ignition is achieved because diesels compress the fuel-air mixture more than an ICE, resulting in temperatures high enough to start combustion.

As you may have guessed this has consequences for the kind of fuel a diesel engine uses. Diesel differs from gasoline in that it is heavier, denser, and less flammable, but also has more energy per gallon. Diesels are often more fuel efficient than ICEs, but they are more expensive and can be harder to start, making them less optimal in colder climates.

Rotary Engine

A rotary engine follows the same four-part cycle of an ICE but is designed such that each part occurs simultaneously. The equivalent of a piston in a rotary engine is a *rotor*, which resembles a triangle with rounded corners and sides. It sits within a rotor housing that contains intake ports, exhaust ports, and spark plugs.

This housing is not cylindrical or spherical, but rather has a somewhat irregular shape like a circle with its north and south poles compressed slightly. The result is that a given rotor side is able to form larger and smaller spaces as it spins. When the rotor passes over the intake valve it forms a larger space which draws in fuel-air mixture. It continues to spin and compresses the fuel-air mixture into a much smaller space, where a spark plug causes combustion. This drives the rotor and causes it to form another open space, with the exhaust generated by combustion being driven out of the exhaust port as that space closes.

When one side of the rotor is entering the compression stage, another side is finishing combustion and still another is beginning intake. There is also usually a second rotor in the same housing which is offset from the first by 180 degrees, meaning combustion is almost always happening.

Each rotor has a hole in the middle into which fits an *eccentric shaft*. The rotors are attached to the eccentric shaft at 180 degrees *to each other*, creating balance, stability, and low amounts of vibration. As in an ICE, the eccentric shaft is what transforms the rotor's rotational motion into the vehicle's propulsive force.

Compared to an ICE rotary engines have far fewer moving parts and generate a lot of power with relatively little size and weight. Their design does give rise to serious challenges with respect to preventing fuel and oil from leaking into places where it doesn't belong. These challenges are met with an intricate series of seals both between a rotor and the housing and between rotors within the same housing.

Duke Engine

In an ICE pistons are attached at right angles to a crankshaft by connecting rods and arranged in a V or inline configuration. Igniting a compressed fuel-air mixture in the cylinder bore generates the power required to move the vehicle. An axial engine — of which the Duke Engine is but one modern incarnation — has its cylinders in a ring and attached to the crankshaft via a star-shaped component called a *reciprocator*. Each piston's connecting rod is attached to one arm of the star, and the collective motion of all the pistons causes the reciprocator to spin. The reciprocator in turn is attached to the crankshaft in such a way that as it rotates the crankshaft spins in the *opposite* direction, with the result being that engine vibration is radically diminished.

Spark plugs and intake/exhaust ports are located on a stationary *head ring* positioned opposite the reciprocator. A spinning piston just starting its four-stroke cycle draws fuel-air mixture into its cylinder bore as it passes over an intake port, compresses it, passes over a spark plug which ignites the fuel-air mixture, expels the exhaust as it passes over an exhaust port, and then begins again.

This piston arrangement allows for the Duke Engine to be much smaller and lighter than an equally-powerful ICE, and with a greater fuel efficiency to boot. It also opens up myriad possibilities for experimenting with applications where the bulk and weight of a traditional engine have been problematic.

Electric Cars

Despite the fact that we have only recently begun to see widespread interest in all-electric vehicles, the technology has been around for a long time. In the mid-nineteenth century Thomas Davenport developed a functioning electric car and Robert Davidson an electric train, though neither were sophisticated enough to replace the non-electric versions of those transportation systems[92]. But electric motors continued to improve, finding applications in commuter trains, railroads, and delivery vehicles, until by the turn of the twentieth century something like 38% of the market was made up of electric vehicles. Alas, Henry Ford's revolutionary manufacturing techniques made gasoline-powered cars affordable enough to knock electric vehicles into the periphery, a position they would occupy up to the present day.

But this hasn't stopped researchers from further studying and improving electric motor design. Today, there are a number of variations on the underlying idea. So-called 'hybrids', for example, use gasoline for highway speeds but switch to electricity when appropriate, such as during idling and at the lower speeds of city commuting. 'Series hybrids' on the other hand always use the electric motor to move the wheels and use a gasoline engine to recharge the electric batteries. All-electric cars do away with gasoline completely.

Notwithstanding the differences between electric and gasoline cars, both solve the problem of providing motive power to wheels. The key differences are in the form this power takes and the way it is distributed. Electric cars use a motor, not an *engine*[93], drawing their power from batteries instead of combustion. This means

---

[92] http://www.explainthatstuff.com/electriccars.html

[93] Drawing the distinction between motors and engines ends up being a fascinating and complex undertaking. See: http://engineering.mit.edu/ask/

that the pistons, cylinder bores, valvetrains, oil, intake manifolds, spark plugs, and other components in a typical internal combustion engine are entirely absent in an electric motor. Moreover, many electric vehicles like the Tesla Model S don't have a transmission[94]. When you accelerate in a standard vehicle you will occasionally feel it lurch a little bit when it shifts into a higher gear. Not so in a Model S, which can accelerate to top speed in a single gear[95].

There are several different ways of getting power from the battery to the wheels. Semi-traditional designs have a motor sitting between either the front or back tires with a gearbox and differentials, which allow the tires to spin at different speeds when the car goes around curves or turns. Others have a motor and a gearbox for each of the front or rear tires, obviating the need for differentials. Still others, like the Mitsubishi MiEV, have a motor for each of the four tires[96]!

As with any new technology, hybrid and electric vehicles have both advantages and disadvantages. The juxtaposition of electric power and gasoline power in hybrids makes them more fuel-efficient, naturally, but they are universally more expensive than their strictly gasoline-powered counterparts and tend to be a bit heavier as well. The purist buying an all-electric car does not escape these disadvantages. Even without any of the machinery required to burn petroleum electric vehicles have heavy Lithium-ion batteries and regenerative brakes. Furthermore, as understood by anyone who has ever screamed in unrelenting fury at a cell phone that dies with 48% of its battery left, battery performance degrades over time. This is especially true in warmer climates, so it may take longer for electric vehicles to penetrate markets in Texas or Arizona.

---

what%E2%80%99s-difference-between-motor-and-engine

[94] The transmission is meant to solve certain problems which are faced by all vehicles, so some electric cars do have transmissions. But the possibilities opened up by electric motors mean it is possible to design vehicles without them.

[95] https://www.youtube.com/watch?v=NaV7V07tEMQ

[96] https://www.youtube.com/watch?v=gnUGvfCkvbk

Defenders of electric vehicles have rightly pointed out that too much has been made of the limited range of electric vehicles. Most people don't drive more than fifty miles a day, so an electric vehicle with a range of 150 miles will generally be more than enough. But people also visit family for the holidays and take road trips, and as yet there isn't a good infrastructure in place for recharging electric vehicles on the road. Someone living in the suburbs or frequently commuting on business must therefore wait until either the range or infrastructure have advanced enough to make an electric vehicle a practical investment.

Rocket Engines

Humans make the journey to space on thrust produced by a fundamentally different kind of engine than the ones discussed above. Whereas those were *rotational* engines whose main function was to produce torque, a *reaction* engine like those found on the Space Shuttle simply create a tremendous amount of force in one direction which allows the payload to move in the opposite direction[97]. Rockets, in other words, are just a means of exploiting Newton's third law of motion: for every action, there is an equal and opposite reaction. One interesting consequence of this fact is that rockets are simultaneously profoundly simple and incredibly elaborate. Almost anyone can assemble a working model rocket in their backyard in a couple of hours. But despite this apparent ease of construction, assembling a functioning rocket is an undertaking of such stupendous complexity that only a few countries have been able to accomplish it.

A common method of explaining rocket engines is to compare them to firehoses. If a fireman were using a water hose while on a skateboard, the basic forces involved would be identical to the ones involved in rocket propulsion. Instead of water, however, rockets tend to burn liquid hydrogen. They are so big, in fact, because they have to have a tremendous amount of fuel in order to get a shuttle or satellite into orbit. And because fuel isn't

---

[97] http://science.howstuffworks.com/rocket.htm

weightless, the more of it a rocket has the more it needs to carry the additional fuel.

NASA's Space Shuttle in probably the image most likely to leap to mind when one hears terms like 'spacecraft' or 'Space Shuttle'.[98]

The orbiter -- the part which looks vaguely like a white airplane -- only weighs about 170,000 pounds[99]. Most of the approximately four-and-a-half million pounds of the Shuttle comes from the fuel in the *external fuel tank* -- the part which looks like a slim, orange grain silo. Attached on either side of the fuel tank are the *solid rocket boosters* which burn with such implacable might that they are able to pierce the atmosphere and propel human beings into the void.

Astonishingly, it takes less time to understand the mechanics of a generic rocket engine than it does internal combustion engines and their myriad variations. There are essentially only a handful of components[100]. The *start* chamber begins the process by creating enough pressure to start a *turbine* connected to a *fuel tank*, which is filled with liquid Hydrogen or Kerosene, and an *oxygen tank*, which contains the oxygen that allows a rocket to function in the vacuum of space.

---

[98]   Image from: http://www.tested.com/science/space/468493-false-starts-astronauts-recall-stories-shuttle-launch-aborts/

[99]   https://www.youtube.com/watch?v=rt5dcrm8X1w

[100]   https://www.youtube.com/watch?v=ln1TDuayllA

The motion of the turbine draws both fuel and oxygen to a *combustion chamber* where they mix and ignite. A small amount of both fuel and oxygen is diverted to a *mixing tank* where they are mixed and ignited again, this time with the purpose of keeping the turbine spinning. The combustion of the fuel/air mixture is what propels the rocket, but here is where things get interesting. Right after the combustion chamber is a *throat*, a restricted aperture through which the ignited fuel must pass. It is this restriction which causes the fuel to accelerate from subsonic to supersonic speeds, in the same way that the water exiting a hose travels faster if you close part of the opening with your thumb. The cone-shaped nozzle gradually increases the amount of space in which the fuel moves as it exits the rocket, creating further acceleration and preventing the shockwaves which might otherwise result.

Of course there are alternative propulsion methods being developed in Heaven as they are on Earth. The relatively new *ion propulsion* technology operates entirely on basic principles of chemistry[101]. The most popular fuel for an ion propulsion system is Xenon, whose aloof refusal to interact with other elements means it is unlikely to behave unpredictably or disturb the other delicate electrical, mechanical, and chemical systems comprised by a spacecraft or satellite.

A *cathode* injects electrons into one end of an *ionization chamber*, and Xenon particles enter on the same side (but not through the cathode). At the opposite end of the chamber are a pair of grids, the internal one carrying a positive charge and the external one carrying a negative charge. The electrons from the cathode are drawn to the positively-charged grid and zoom toward it, knocking loose electrons from the Xenon atoms as they do. The resulting positively-charged Xenon ions make their way toward the far end of the ionization chamber, passing through the positively-charged grid as they do. At this point they are massively accelerated by their attraction to the negatively-charged grid and forcefully shot out of the ionization chamber into space, creating thrust.

---

[101] https://www.youtube.com/watch?v=grU8g9jnS4w

Problems might arise if the 'exhaust' of this process consisted entirely of Xenon ions, which might turn around and accelerate back *toward* the negatively-charged grid to which they were drawn in the first place. To prevent this an additional cathode is affixed to some outside part of the ionization chamber, firing electrons into the wake and thus neutralizing the Xenon ions.

Ion propulsion is very slow to accelerate, but the process is extremely fuel efficient because Xenon has a high specific impulse -- the ratio of thrust produced per unit fuel -- and the top speed eventually reached exceeds that of chemical rockets, at least in theory. At present ionization is mostly used to make small corrections keep satellites where they're supposed to be[102]. But there are several different higher-power ion propulsion systems currently undergoing testing which might someday allow this technology to play a bigger role in space exploration and settlement missions.

---

[102] https://www.nasa.gov/centers/glenn/about/fs21grc.html

Chapter 12
As the World Opens

Why had she always felt that joyous sense of confidence when look-ing at machines?—she thought. In these giant shapes, two aspects pertaining to the inhuman were radiantly absent: the causeless and the purposeless. Every part of the motors was an embodied answer to 'Why?' and 'What for?'—like the steps of a life-course chosen by the sort of mind she worshipped. The motors were a moral code cast in steel.

They are alive, she thought, because they are the physical shape of the action of a living power—of the mind that had been able to grasp the whole of this complexity, to set its purpose, to give it form. For an instant, it seemed to her that the motors were transparent and she was seeing the net of their nervous system. It was a net of connections, more intricate, more crucial than all of their wires and circuits: the rational connections made by that human mind which had fashioned any one part of them for the first time.

—Atlas Shrugged, Ayn Rand

In the classic film American Beauty there is a famous scene where-in one character shows another a video of a plastic bag as it's blown about by the wind. In whispers he describes how beautiful he found the experience of watching it as it danced, and amidst platitudes about 'a benevolent force' he notes that this was the day he fully learned that there is a hidden universe behind the objects which most people take for granted.

One of the chief benefits of The STEMpunk Project has been that it has reinforced this experience in me. While I have thoroughly enjoyed gaining practical knowledge of gears, circuits, and CPUs, perhaps the greater joy has come from a heightened awareness of the fact that the world is shot through with veins of ingenuity and depth.

Understanding the genesis of this awareness requires a brief detour into psychology. Many people seem to labor under the impression that perception happens in the sense organs. Light or sound from an object hits someone and that person observes the object. Cognitive science shows definitively that this is not the case. Perception happens in the brain, and sensory data are filtered heavily through the stock of concepts and experiences within the observer. This is why an experienced mechanic can listen to a malfunctioning engine and hear subtle clues which point to one possible underlying cause or another where I only hear a vague rattling noise.

As my conceptual toolkit increases, therefore, I can expect to perceive things that were invisible to me before I had such knowledge. And this has indeed been the case. More than once I have found myself passing some crystallized artifact of thought — like a retaining wall, or an electrical substation — and wondering how it was built. That this question occurs to me at all is one manifestation of a new perspective on the infrastructure of modern life which is by turns fascinating, humbling, and very rewarding.

Let me illustrate with the example of the washer, which you may know as these things:

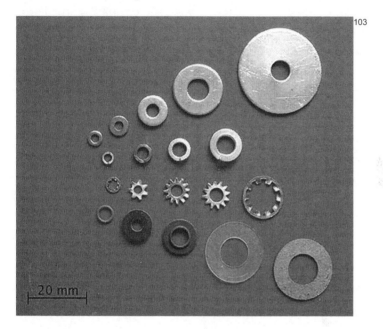

103

20 mm

A washer is a small metal disc with a hole in its middle like a doughnut, and they are so ubiquitous that it's nearly impossible to have done much tinkering without having encountered one. They are often found wherever a threaded fastener like a screw or a bolt is being used to bind multiple objects together. On many occasions, after having disassembled something I have dutifully put the washers back in place without having really understood their purpose.

People sometimes use the term 'washer' to describe the gaskets used in plumbing to stop unwanted water leakage, but washers do a variety of things besides acting as seals. Perhaps the most important is that they work to evenly distribute force and load.

Imagine that you're fastening two boards together with a screw. Getting a really tight fit means drilling the screw as far as possible into the board. As the screw head, still turning, comes into contact

---

103   https://en.wikipedia.org/wiki/Washer_(hardware)

with the top board a tremendous amount of torque is generated. Many a novice carpenter has watched in dismay as a screw placed near the end of a board causes a nasty split in the wood, introducing a source of weakness. But placing a washer between the screw head and board greatly reduces the chances of such splitting because the torque is spread out over the larger, harder surface area of the metal disc.

Now imagine that you've used bolts to fasten a short board to a long board and have hung an equal weight from both ends of the long board. Where is all the resulting downward force concentrated? In the small area covered by the bolt as it exits the board! With a small amount of weight this isn't going to be a problem, but it can become one as weight increase. The most common solution I have seen is to place a washer on the exit side and to use a nut to secure it in place. Here, the washer is both distributing the load of the weights and distributing the torque of the nut as it's being tightened into place.

Why is it necessary to fasten things together so tightly that we risk splitting a board? In part because forces that aren't of much consequence when making a bookshelf become extremely important when building a deck or chassis. As a vehicle runs it vibrates, and any bolts in the engine or body will begin to shake loose. As a deck weathers multiple seasons the wood of which it is made expands and contracts, compromising the integrity of the joints holding it together. If this shifting is extreme enough something important might break loose, causing injury or death.

With this in mind there are washer variants designed to keep even more tension on fasteners and joints. Star washers are built with teeth which bite into their point of contact, making them harder to dislodge. Belleville, wave, and curved washers all deform slightly when they are tightened down, increasing the pressure at the joint in a manner similar to how a compressed spring might.

This isn't all that washers do. They can also be used as a kind of adapter whenever a bolt is too small for a hole, as spacers if a bolt happens to be too long, as boundaries between two metals like aluminum and steel whose contact will result in corrosion, and as electrical insulators.

***

I have begun to see and appreciate the symmetry of guard rails on a staircase, the system of multicolored pipes carrying electricity and water through a building, the lattice of girders and beams holding up a bridge; each one the mark of a conscious intelligence, each one a frozen set of answers to a long string of 'whys' and 'hows'.

This notion can be pushed further: someone has to make not just the beams, but also the machinery that helps to make the beams, and the machinery which mines the materials to make the beams, and the machinery which makes the trucks which carries raw materials and finished products to where they are needed, like ripples in a fabric of civilization pulsing across the world.

It's gorgeous.

A corollary to the preceding is an increased confidence in my own ability to understand how things work, and with it a more robust sense of independent agency. For most of my life I have been a very philosophical person: I like symbols and abstractions, math, music, and poetry. But if every nut and bolt in my house was placed there in accordance with the plans of a human mind, then as the possessor of a (reasonably high-functioning) human mind I ought to be able to puzzle out the basic idea.

Don't misunderstand me: I know very well that poking around in a breaker box without all the appropriate precautions in place could get me killed. I still approach actual physical systems carefully. But I like to sit in an unfinished basement and trace the path from electrical outlet to conduit to box to subpanel to main panel. On occasion I even roll up my sleeves and actually fix things, albeit after doing a lot of research first.

In fact, you can do a similar exercise right now, wherever you are, to experience some of what I'm describing without going through the effort of The STEMpunk Project. Chances are if you're reading this you're in a room, probably one built with modern techniques by a contractor's crew.

Set a timer on your phone for five minutes, and simply look around you. Perhaps your computer is sitting on a table or a desk. What kind of wood is the desk made out of? Were the legs and top machine-made or crafted by hand? If it has a rolling top, imagine how difficult it must have been for the person who made the first prototype.

Does the room have carpet or hardwood floors? Have you ever seen the various materials that go under carpets? Could you lay carpet, if you needed to replace a section? Are different materials used beneath carpet and beneath hardwood? If so, why?

You're probably surrounded by four walls. Look at where they meet the floor. Is there trim at the seam? What purpose does it serve, and how was it installed so tightly? Most people know that behind their walls there are evenly-spaced boards called 'studs'. Who figured out the optimum amount of space between studs? How do you locate studs when you want to hang a picture or a poster on your wall? Probably with a device called a stud finder. How did men find studs before the stud finder was invented?

Does the ceiling above you lay flat or rise up to a point? If it's a point, have you ever wondered how builders get the point of the ceiling directly over the center of the room? Sure, they probably took measurements of the length and width of the room and did some simple division to figure out where the middle lies. But actually cutting boards and rafters and arranging them so that they climb to an apex directly over the room's midpoint is much harder than it sounds.

If you do this enough you'll hopefully find that the mundane and quotidian are surprisingly beautiful in their own way. Well-built things, even just dishwashers and ceiling fans, possess an order and exactness to rival that of the greatest symphonies.

I'm glad I learned to see it.

Appendix A
Notes on Magical Style

Throughout this book I've made liberal use of poetic, thaumaturgi-cal, and mythical language in discussions of topics that are entirely scientific and technological. After posting the following excerpt to Facebook:

'It seems clear that the logical conclusion of voice-, gesture-, and thought-recognition software is a magical user interface (MUI). What is 'wingardium leviosa' but a verbal command? What are tight, precise wand movements but gesture-based computing? And when your favorite song comes on the moment you want to hear it is there any practical difference between that and casting a spell? If we as-sume that magical systems are rule-based technologies with vari-ous methods of providing input then the drive to create smaller, less visible, more fluid ways of working with our devices could result in a future that resembles the worlds we love to read about. Arthur C. Clarke's famous maxim that 'any sufficiently advanced technology is indistinguishable from magic' was as precient in 1962 as it is now. But this way, the underlying mechanisms will be comprehensible to anyone willing to do their own STEMpunk Project.'

I received this criticism:

'Respectfully, I disagree a lot—with both of the points made in this excerpt. Your main point is that if we can get an interface that seems like magic, we have replicated magic. Okay. Yes, that would be very convenient, but what distinguishes Harry Potter magic/fan-tasy magic is not the interface, but the effect. When a wizard waves his wand he can levitate something or shrink a person to a different

size—our machines will never be able to do many of the things that fantasy magic can do. Making an intuitive interface and calling it magic is the ultimate over-promise.

Your lesser point is the Clarke quote, which I'll admit is one of my pet peeves. Clarke wrote that because he did not have any knowledge of what is historically considered 'magic' or how people believe it's done. Sure, sufficiently advanced technology may or may not seem supernatural to a less advanced culture, but actual cultures draw a firm line between what they call magic and what they call advanced technology. A favorite example: in the ancient Middle East, there is evidence that a crude form of electroplating was used, and obviously the way this process worked was a complete mystery to them. Yet we have records of their magical rituals, talismans and beliefs; their magic system does not involve or look similar to their metal-plating technology. The same could be said for metallurgy in ancient northern Europe, which operated on mysterious principles and had mystical associations, but was seen as completely different from their large body of magical rituals and spells. Equating magic and technology is perhaps the single most common mistake I see fellow science-lovers make—mostly because we tend to be as ignorant about magical traditions as magic-believers are about science.'

These objections are worth answering.

First, a quibble: my claim was not that the magic was in the *interface* per se, but rather that the combination of extremely advanced technology along with a fluid, intuitive interface would render a world suffused with forces *indistinguishable* from the kind of magic we might find in the fantasy genre. Some combination of smart matter, nanotechnology, ultra-light materials, and miniscule propulsion might eventually yield objects that can levitate. If we add voice-recognition software which responds to 'wingardium leviosa' then we've surely replicated that particular spell with enough fidelity to satisfy anyone who doesn't have an engineer-grade interest in the mechanisms involved.

My critic goes on to note that it's not the *wand* which makes the magic, but the effect. He is probably right that there are some things, like shrinking a human being down to a minute size, which a fictional wizard can do but a scientist probably never will -- I don't see how, even in principle, a person's underlying metabolic and cognitive processes could be preserved at 10 percent of the body's normal size. But that argument can be applied in reverse: I'm unaware of any magical equivalent of recursively-self-improvement superintelligences, dyson spheres, or Von Neumann probes. Does Harry Potter have a spell which would allow him to implement an agent able to learn to make medical diagnoses better than any living human doctor?

I concede his point that ancient magic-based cultures drew sharp distinctions between mystical enterprise and mysterious technology; this is correct as far as I know. So why compare electronic circuits to a 'light mandala' when electricity isn't light and circuits aren't mandalas? Because it's the only way I know to project and kindle the appropriate emotional response to the achievements of the modern world. To paraphrase Douglas Adams, people seem to:

1) take for granted the technology present when they're born as simply a part of the way things are;

2) become excited by things invented before they're thirty-five;

3) thereafter view developments with grumpy vexation.

Supercomputers might be impressive in a vague sort of way, but who realizes that plain 'ol desktops are miraculous too? Smooth touch-screen interfaces might briefly warrant a grin, but does anyone pause even momentarily to notice how much goes into the construction of a simple yellow pencil?

In truth I usually don't excel in this regard either; I can't begin to describe how furious I get when my cell phone dies with 48 percent of its battery remaining. But in my better moments I'm awestruck at the incomprehensible vastness of what man's mind has built. And the best expressive vehicle culture seems to have produced for conveying 'incomprehensible vastness' is largely religious and magical.

So those are the tools I used.

47422277R00090

Made in the USA
San Bernardino, CA
12 August 2019